IN MY OWN WORDS

Nicholasa Mohr

Growing Up
Inside the Sanctuary
of My Imagination

Julian (M) Messner
Published by Simon & Schuster
New York   London   Toronto   Sydney   Tokyo   Singapore

YA- B
MOH

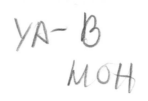

JULIAN MESSNER
Published by Simon & Schuster
1230 Avenue of the Americas
New York, NY 10020.

JULIAN MESSNER and colophon
are trademarks of Simon & Schuster
Book design by Sylvia Frezzolini
Manufactured in the United States of America.

10 9 8 7 6 5 4 3 2 1

Library of Congress Cataloging-in-Publication Data
Mohr, Nicholasa.
In my own words : growing up inside the sanctuary of my imagination / Nicholasa Mohr.
p.   cm.
1. Mohr, Nicholasa—Childhood and youth—Juvenile literature.   2. Women authors,
American—20th century—Biography—Juvenile literature.   3. Puerto Ricans—New York
(N.Y.)—Social life and customs—Juvenile literature.   [1. Nohr, Nicholasa.   2. Authors,
American.   3. Women—Biography.   4. Puerto Ricans—Biography.]   I. Title.
PS3563.036Z466   1994   813'.54—dc20   [B]   93-34685   CIP   AC

ISBN 0-671-74171-3

For Betty Barnett, Elia Hidalgo Christensen, and Hilda Hidalgo, with gratitude for those intervals when my life took tragic and irrevocable turns, and you were always there, generous and loving. And for sharing the good times, too.

Contents

. . . .

	Introduction *vii*
One	Earliest Memories *1*
Two	Conflicts and Family Secrets *7*
Three	Born Female and Lucky to be Last *13*
Four	The Magic of Pictures and Words *20*
Five	Summertime Freedom *30*
Six	Kindergarten *36*
Seven	Christmas Came with Joy and Plenty *42*
Eight	Surprises, More Farewells, and Things Change *46*
Nine	Freedom to Learn and Reflections on Religion *61*
Ten	Deaths in the Family *70*
Eleven	A Teacher Cares *76*

Twelve   A Social Worker's Wrath and
                      Mother's Fortitude 79

Thirteen   Making Up and Shedding Enemies 84

Fourteen   The Matriarchy Governs 90

Fifteen   Sadness and Disappointment
                      Go Hand in Hand 98

Sixteen   Graduation and the Final Good-bye 107

              Epilogue 112

              Published Works 116

Introduction

When I was first asked to write this book, I hesitated. I was not interested in writing an autobiography that would focus primarily on a chronicle of facts and a sequence of events.

My editor, Adriane Ruggiero, told me that I was not bound to write this book in any particular manner. I then explained to her the kind of book I wanted to author.

My intent was to write a memoir that would examine and explore the creative process that had fired me on when I was growing up, and to show how this process helped me to endure, to overcome, and to succeed. Upon mutual agreement, contracts were signed and I began my work on this book.

I searched my memories and selected incidents that would reveal how imagination and creative thinking had a significant impact on my behavior and my development.

This is not so much a book about the importance of characters and circumstances as it is about revealing my own private reality as a child. This exclusive reality enabled me to survive and eventually push myself beyond the confines of my troubled world. It granted me the freedom to flourish.

In my attempts to be honest and forthright, I have expressed my opinions and conclusions without reservations. Therefore, I have chosen in some instances, with the exception of family members, to leave out or change the names of some of the people that I write about in this book.

I do not feel that actual names are of any great importance, since this is a real story about my emotions, my beliefs, and my search for self-esteem while growing up female, Puerto Rican, and poor in these United States. Names and minor, mundane details are extraneous to the core and the purpose of this account of my young life. I am satisfied that I have dealt with what was essential in this undertaking.

There is a school of thought that maintains that a good memory is an asset for writers. This was certainly true when I was writing my story, because it was fairly easy to recall my early life. I have always had a good memory and still remember most of the incidents and circumstances as they occurred in my young years.

Let me give another example of the importance of memory in my writing. My ability to remember an incident that I had found intriguing in the past has often been the basis for a story or a novel. In writing fiction, I nurture this idea and bring my imagination to play in the development of a narrative.

However, in the case of this memoir, I had to stay focused on the reality of my life and challenge my imagination to explore the causes for my behavior. Truth and the power of my creative life became my focus as I relived those pivotal stages of evolution during my childhood.

I would also like to share with my readers that unexpectedly, in dealing with these intimate beliefs, I enlightened my own consciousness and healed some of my latent wounds. A writer on occasion will say that writing a particular work was a "cathartic experience." Such was the case while I worked on this book.

I chose to end my story at the time of my mother's death, when I was fourteen and a half years old. This concludes an era of innocence for me and was truly the culmination of my coming of age. In my epilogue, I supply further information as to the subsequent development of my life and career.

I wish to thank my brother George for his friendship, and for helping me locate the few remaining family photographs that have been reproduced in this book.

AWAKENINGS

Awakenings in my soul!
Awakenings in my mind!
When the intimate door
opens to give entry into oneself,
what awakenings!

From *Amaneceres* by Julia De Burgos;
translated from the Spanish
by Miriam Jiménez Román

One
·······
Earliest Memories

*I*n my earliest memories of thinking and deciding, I am being pushed in a stroller. Sweet orange juice flows through my mouth and down into my stomach as I suck on the nipple of my baby bottle.

Up above is a long stretch of sky framed on either side by tenement buildings that are four or five stories tall. An assortment of people are looking out open windows or sitting on their fire escapes. The metal fire escapes appear like black lace and trimming on brick cloth. These people share their sitting space with plants and flowers spilling out of flowerpots. They must ease themselves around the clotheslines strung along the metal bars so as not to disturb the laundry drying in the bright sunshine.

Along the street, traffic flows while kids screaming and playing dodge cars, trucks, bicycles and one another. The sidewalks and stoop steps are swarming with children and adults. I feel like I am being pushed through a wall of bodies.

The horde of humanity is everywhere. Noise, so much clamor. I try to turn it off, but no matter how much I try the noise is everywhere.

Only when I look up, high up, do I get a glimpse of serenity as white clouds sail gracefully along the wide blue sky. Pigeons fly in groups, swirling, vanishing, and then reappearing.

Up there, I point . . . I want to be up there, where there is space, where I can breathe, and where it is quiet so I can think and dream.

I try to explain to my mother, but I can't really form words yet or communicate with speech. I babble forcefully. She stops the stroller and warns me to sit still or I'll get a smack. My mother is afraid I'll fall out and hurt myself. And so I settle back again, suck for more orange juice, cup my hand so that the bright sun does not smart my eyes, and gaze upward, trying to search as far as I can into the vast sky. I continue searching for space, for quiet, for a chance to think and a chance to imagine.

That was when I first learned that although I could not shut the noise out of my ears I could somehow, like magic, erase the noise from my mind.

Stillness enveloped me as I focused on the wide sky with its blue background. White clouds outlined by golden sunlight sped by, unpredictably changing shapes. From giant forms to mere puffs, the clouds separated and joined together, always different and surprising. In this mood of quiet bliss I fell fast asleep, to voyage into a state of tranquility, leaving pandemonium far away.

It was the first time I remember slipping consciously into the world of my imagination.

When I awoke at home back in my crib, I realized that the possibilities of such adventures into a realm of inspired thought could prove to be quite wonderful.

After that, I knew I wanted to be in another place and that someday I would leave my crowded environment. Somehow even before I could speak, I knew that I could not stay to endure life in this chaos and forfeit my private space. There were too many things to think about and too many escapades to consider, and for that I would need to have distance from others.

That crowded street was my block and it was located in *El Barrio,* known as Spanish Harlem, on Manhattan's Upper East Side. At that time, in 1940, we lived on East 100th Street between Madison and Park avenues.

Our apartment was on the fourth floor of a tenement building. We had a five-room railroad flat. It was called "railroad" because the rooms ran right into one another without a foyer or hallway to separate them. There was a fire escape facing the back, a kitchen, and one bathroom, followed by three small connecting rooms. The largest room faced the front and doubled as a bedroom and living room.

In the first five years of my life, we moved several times, always within a ten-block radius. Each new apartment was a similar railroad flat, just about the same size and shape as the one we had just vacated. That's why it never took me more than a day or two to adjust.

I shared my home with six older brothers and my parents, as well as with my mother's older sister, Aunt Maria, who was a widow, and her eleven-year-old son, Ralphy. Aunt Maria and Ralphy had arrived from Puerto Rico a few months before I turned three.

My aunt suffered from epileptic seizures. Although they occurred infrequently, she took strong medication and was not always able to work. She became hard of hearing, either from the medication or from her seizures, and would never wear a hearing aid. After a bad fall, she ruptured her intestines and, after a number of operations, became incapacitated and received a small disability pension.

As Aunt Maria got older, she became more and more eccentric. Sometimes her eccentricities caused arguments, at other times the episodes were humorous.

She accused family members of stealing her handmade handkerchiefs and items of clothing that she kept locked up in a trunk.

"Why would anyone want your handkerchiefs or clothes?" my mother would say, trying to reason with Aunt Maria. But it did no good. My aunt had padlocks on her closet and on numerous suitcases where she kept her possessions. She wore a long keychain around her neck that held all of her keys. I always knew when she was near because of the jingling of the metal keys.

Most of the time she held on to her pocketbook, and even during meals she never let it out of her sight. Often when we had visitors she would begin to hide the few items of silver we owned, much to my mother's embarrassment. Most of the guests were good-natured and merely laughed (it was rather funny to see her skulking about, hiding candlesticks and trays), but there were others who were insulted by her behavior.

If my mother in any way admonished my aunt, she would become furious. Aunt Maria had a nasty temper, and she would rant and accuse my mother and everyone else in the family of abusing her.

At one time or another, just about every person at home lost their patience with Aunt Maria and argued with her. Consequently that person would be subjected to one of her scathing tirades. These moments of rage disappeared as quickly as they emerged, and soon all was forgotten and forgiven.

On the other hand, when she wasn't paranoid, Aunt Maria was sweet, considerate, and totally devoted to all of us, as well as very hardworking. We all accepted her eccentricities as a fact of everyday life. This was who she was, and we all loved her very much.

I used to sit on her lap, and she would sing songs to me and tell me about when she was a little girl in Puerto Rico. Sometimes she cooked a special dessert for me or quietly pressed a penny or two into the palm of my hand.

I never knew any of my grandparents, and my aunt Maria was the closest I ever got to having a grandmother.

Ralphy grew up as if he were my brother; my parents treated him as they did their own sons. He went to school and quickly learned English. In no time he was just like any other kid in our neighborhood.

Even though my apartment was crowded when the adults were home from work and the kids home from school, I felt safe there. I had my designated space with my own small bed with crib guards. Everyone was family, familiar faces I loved and trusted.

I remember thinking how expansive everything seemed to me

then, as I crawled around under tables and chairs and climbed the countless folding cots, bunk beds, and daybeds. All the sleeping accommodations were neatly folded and covered over with slipcovers. One would hardly know that ten people lived in such a small space.

To me at such a tender age, the rooms appeared enormous. As an adult, when I visited one of these apartments I was astonished to see how narrow the space really is and how small the rooms are.

Perhaps my amazement was partly because my earliest, most formative years had been molded in such a confined environment. Yet my memories of this limited space recounted experiences that often stretched my imagination and transported me to the threshold of my creativity, where my domain was too vast to measure.

Two
·········
Conflicts and Family Secrets

*L*ike many large families, we had our share of problems and arguments within our home. My mother, who was born in Ponce, Puerto Rico, had married at age sixteen and by twenty-three had borne four boys. Her marriage was one of misery and brutality. She had been orphaned at twelve and had no one to offer her shelter and protection.

I am still amazed at my mother's strength, that as such a young person she managed to save and successfully plan her departure from her abusive husband. My mother entrusted the care of her children to her married older sister Maria and her husband. Then she booked a one-way ticket on a steamer and sailed to New York City in 1929. She told me that leaving her babies was one of the saddest days of her life.

Once in New York, she joined another married sister, Regina, and her husband, who had been living in the city for two years. Except for her fine needlework, my mother had no working skills, but with their help she was able to find a job.

After working for two years as an unskilled worker in the laundries and garment sweatshops of New York City, my mother still had not saved enough money to send for her young sons.

At work, she met Don Pedro, a bachelor eighteen years her senior who had no children of his own. After a short courtship, they set up house, and he sent for her children.

They were married, and Don Pedro adopted her boys as his own. My mother bore him two sons, and then I was born.

From an early age I remember accusations and countless arguments between my parents. They revolved around the circumstances of my birth. My mother was accused of having had an affair, and I was supposed to be the offspring of this alleged liaison.

However, I remember my mother's forceful denials, her tears, and her rage. Up until her death, my mother always denied this accusation.

The other man in question, who for the sake of discretion I shall call Martin, had always been in the picture. Prior to my birth and during my first year of life he had been our boarder, and subsequently our neighbor. He was considered a close family friend.

This was an ongoing dilemma that brought about our family's disruption. Before I was four years of age my parents went through several separations.

Once my mother left her husband and took us all to live in a small furnished apartment. I can recall how we were all packed into two rooms. My mother had to cook on a hot plate and we had no refrigerator.

During another separation, a custody battle ensued and I was secretly sent off to live with one of my mother's friends, Edie. Edie had a son about my own age. I was not allowed to leave their apartment or to look out the windows. I remember high ceilings, soft rugs on wooden floors, and peeking out of drawn shades into an alleyway where stray cats searched for food among the trash bins.

Time for a child is continual; a moment can seem like a full chapter in one's life. As an adult, the recollection of just one day of childhood can often emerge in the mind as an endless span of time. So I never knew how long these separations were. But later on I was told that they never lasted more than two or three weeks and that my visit at Edie's was no more than a few days.

My memory is that at some point things became calm, my parents reconciled, and whether he believed it or not, ostensibly my father accepted me as his natural daughter.

By the time my parents had their last and final reconciliation, Martin was out of our lives. I was told it was the only way for my mother and father to maintain a peaceful existence and keep the family intact.

While my father was serious and hardworking, Martin was irresponsible and never held a job. He was an ex-bootlegger and a gambler by trade, who loved to drink and chase women. *Un mujeriego y un sinverquenza.* A no-good woman chaser, with little dignity, was how he was described.

I did not know what those things meant and cared nothing for other's opinions about Martin.

I only knew that there was always a treat for me from Martin, and he often left pocket change in my hand. "For my princess to buy herself some candy . . ."

When we played cards, I always won. He'd cook my favorite foods and give me all the ice cream I wanted.

Although I never saw Martin on a daily basis, we had formed a strong bond. I adored him; he was my special friend who added tenderness and love to my life.

He made a fuss when I sang or danced and acted astonished at every picture I drew. "These drawings should be in museums!" he would exclaim, even when I didn't know what a museum was.

In Martin's eyes I could do no wrong. I was beautiful and I was smart. This unconditional love did not come to me from my mother or father, but it was always given by Martin.

I had even been allowed to visit with him and stay overnight from time to time. My last overnight visit with Martin was when I was just six, and it shines in my memory as a perfect example of the essence of our attachment.

Martin had fallen on hard times and gambled away all of his money and worldly possessions. He had rented a dark basement apartment with a makeshift kitchen.

Yet that afternoon, when we arrived at his apartment, it had several vases filled with yellow roses. To this day the yellow rose is my favorite flower. A table complete with tablecloth and napkins was set for two. The aroma of Puerto Rican-style *arroz con pollo,* my favorite dish, permeated the apartment.

Before we could eat, Martin said he had a very important story to tell. First, he asked me what part of the chicken I preferred. I laughed, because he knew that my favorite part was the thigh and leg.

"All right," he said, and set down not one or two, but six thighs and legs on my plate. This amazed me because this was before the supermarket era when people could buy their favorite chicken parts in large frozen packs. In those days, whole chickens were sold and only cut up into pieces by the local butcher upon the customer's request.

Martin told me the story of how he had to travel long and far into the state of New Jersey, to visit a farmer who had a chicken with six legs.

"You don't know what I went through so that he would sell me that six-legged chicken!" he declared quite dramatically. Martin explained how he had begged and pleaded and told the old farmer that he was giving an important dinner for this very special little girl. "A talented artist," he had assured him. Martin even promised to give the farmer one of my drawings. Only then did he convince the old farmer to let him have the six-legged chicken. Of course I then agreed to make a special drawing for Martin in order to replace the one he had given to the reluctant farmer.

I laughed at his audacious story, since I knew that chickens only had two legs and that he must be making the whole thing up. Yet I never questioned Martin. Instead I listened attentively to his every word. I became part of the fantasy and reveled in the pretending because I knew it was Martin's way of enchanting me. So I clapped and roared with laughter when he imitated the six-legged chicken, and upon his request agreed to draw a portrait of the deceased fowl.

I sipped grape juice out of my long-stemmed wineglass and watched as Martin emptied the large bottle of wine into his own glass. We ate till we couldn't manage another bite, then we played cards. Of course, I won all the games.

Finally, Martin lay down on the bed fully clothed and fell fast asleep in a happy intoxicated stupor. I put on my pajamas, found the blankets, covered him over, and lay down, putting my hand on his heaving chest to feel the deep vibrations of his breath.

I snuggled up close and examined his face, running my small fingers over his cheekbones, his almond-shaped eyes, and his open mouth as it emitted a steady snore. The rhythmic reverberations of his snoring soon made me sleepy. I lay beside Martin, feeling well fed, absolutely adored, and saturated with contentment. I was cradled by his love and the magic of his imagination. As my eyelids began to close, I remember thinking that I could not envision ever being any happier.

This was to be our last visit together. In order for there to be peace at home, Martin had to be out of the picture. When I saw him again, several years later, it was to be a sad chapter in my life.

Innuendos among family members concerning my mother's disloyalty were never really put to rest.

These rumors often caused disruption and violence. The day that my oldest brother, Johnny, announced that he was leaving home, I witnessed a bitter quarrel. Among the most terrible exchanges I ever saw take place between Johnny and my father was when my father denied me as his birth daughter. Johnny then accused him of being less than a man and cursed his existence. My father struck Johnny and a fight broke out. Behind a partially opened door, I watched horrified as fists flew and blood splattered. It took all the rest of my family to pull them apart.

"I hate you and I'll never come back to live here!" my brother screamed, and he never did.

Three
....

Born Female and Lucky
to be Last

I was the youngest of seven children and the only female. I was an "accident" and an unwelcome pregnancy.

After having six sons, my mother had given up all hope of having a girl and was despondent during most of her pregnancy. Years later, I remembered hearing one of my aunts say that my mother's despair had come out of her deception. Only my mother could have responded to the accuracy of such a statement.

Although the Great Depression was slowly ending in 1938, times were still hard and the majority of people were out of work.

I was perceived as yet another mouth to feed for my family, and had I been a male child, my reception into this world would have been ambivalent at best.

On the day of my birth, my mother refused to leave her children with anyone, claiming it was not yet time. My mom decided that going to the hospital with her seventh child, especially after two previous miscarriages, was not necessary. She figured that a midwife would do just as well for this routine birth.

But when her water broke, complications resulted. I was to

13

be a breech baby, born feet first. The hospital was called and several doctors replaced the midwife. Later on, my mother told me she had undergone forty-eight hours of labor.

"You were my most difficult birth, but having my little girl made it all worthwhile."

My mother told me that after my birth, when people remarked how cute or pretty I was, she always told them that I could look like a monkey and she would still think I was beautiful.

"After six sons, I've finally got my daughter," she told them. According to her, she had always wanted a girl. I believe she was telling the truth because after me there were no more children.

Even though I was born into a poor family, female, and of Puerto Rican parents who lived in a society rampant with racism and xenophobia, I've always felt lucky. Even growing up with the mystery as to who my real father was could not make me less grateful.

Some higher powers beyond mortality had mercifully decided not to stack all the cards against me: they allowed me to be born the last child in my family. Had I been born first or even third or fourth, my life could easily have been one of servitude.

As can be the tradition in Puerto Rican and/or Latino cultures, many households are male dominated. As a female I would have been bound to take care of my brothers. Cooking, cleaning, baby-sitting, and tending to those who are sick would have consumed my young life.

My own dreams and goals might never have been taken seriously since, as the oldest female, my duties would most likely already have been defined for me. The thought of such an existence still makes me shudder.

But destiny allowed me to linger in the land of the unborn until I arrived as the *la nena de la familia,* the baby girl of our family, at a time when my oldest brothers were already in high school.

Consequently, there was to be no older-sister status or substitute-mother role for me. I've always been thankful for this luck of fate.

As a girl, I was a novelty in a family of so many males and a great joy to my mother, Nicolasa.

I was named after my mother. Except there is an *h* in my name, which is spelled Nicholasa. This happened because the clerk registered Nicolasa with an *h* after the *c,* giving it an Anglo spelling.

As a native of this city that has a long history of immigration, and like so many before me, my name was given a different spelling. I've never minded this bureaucratic arrogance because it also anointed my name with a New York flavor.

My dad worked as a laborer six days a week and put in as much overtime as he could get. He was a dedicated union man and a committed Socialist, loudly anticlerical, cursing the church every chance he got.

My mother was a Roman Catholic, but her religious rituals always paid deference to *El Espiritismo,* the spiritualism practiced in Puerto Rico and in some areas of the Caribbean. The roots of *El Espiritismo* arrived from West Africa and were combined with the religious beliefs of the Roman Catholic church.

Early in my life I began to appreciate that spiritual and cultural enrichment of my African-Caribbean heritage.

My mother would take me with her occasionally when she visited *El Centro de Espiritismo,* seeking counsel from the *curanderos.* After a consultation, the mediums and religious leaders gave her prayers to recite and herbs, incense, and candles to light, all in conjunction with Catholic rites.

At home she prayed faithfully in front of her sacred altar. Her altar was arranged on a shelf where she usually placed a holy picture of a saint (her two most esteemed saints were St. Jude and St. Lazarus), a glass of water, a string of beads, an offering of fruit, and a lit candle in a small red glass holder.

My mother loved plants and flowers. She grew a variety of plants in flowerpots, including an assortment of herbs. Peppermint, chamomile, sage are a few of the herbs I remember. Whenever she had a little extra money, my mother would buy fresh flowers for her altar (lilacs were her favorite spring flowers).

My parents were always arguing about religion and politics. Their debates became a source of fascination for me. I got to hear two very different points of view.

My father was an avowed atheist, and his pragmatic approach to all things helped give me a balanced view of my personal circumstances.

My mother was not truly a devout, practicing Catholic. For example, she seldom went to confession and preferred worshiping at her altar to going to Sunday mass. Her visits to church had to do with novenas and *promesas,* promises that she had negotiated on her own. Thus, she felt that it was more effective to deal directly with God and the saints instead of dealing with the priests.

It was her spiritual life that was important to her, and she believed in the power of God, the Virgin Mary, and the saints of the Roman Catholic church as distinguished by *El Espiritismo*.

While my father felt sorry for his wife and her "religious and superstitious beliefs," my mother prayed for her ignorant husband's soul.

In fact, my parents' opposed points of view caused me to contemplate their distinct beliefs seriously. I believe these exchanges encouraged me to read further so that I could eventually seek out my own truth.

That experience has served me well, for to this day I can empathize with both sides and have learned to celebrate my own relationship to humankind.

To earn extra money, my mother and Aunt Maria took in homework, assembling plastic flowers and other novelties or sewing fancy borders on napkins and tablecloths. At night, huge boxes were set in the living room and kitchen while all the kids gathered around to help with the piecework. I don't remember how much we were paid, but I knew it amounted to no more than a few dollars per workload.

My brothers were all going to school, and from a very early age, I had to learn to amuse myself. When Martin was part of our family I saw him quite often. And before my parents' final reconciliation, there had been the occasional overnight visits with Martin. Sometimes on weekends different relatives visited with their children. I was always happy to play with my cousins. However, most days during the daytime, except for my mom (and sometimes my aunt), everyone was either working or in school.

My days were spent indoors, inside our railroad flat where the rooms were empty of people. I would see my horizon as the walls and ceilings, with two windows at either end of the apartment. These windows provided me with my only view of the outside world.

Four stories high and no place to go, no backyard or porch. That outside world just beyond my touch existed in another reality.

When I reached up to the windowsill and looked outside, I saw other buildings that looked just like ours. Scraggly trees competed for sunshine with clotheslines that were loaded with people's underwear and work garments. The long clotheslines zigzagged throughout the backyards, extending far as the eye could see. Sparrows chirped and nested in the tree branches or hopped onto electric-pole wires, while squirrels leaped and chased one another from tree limbs to rooftops.

In the early 1940s, television was not yet a part of the American household. We did have two radios, but they were always reserved for the grown-ups.

During the daytime I had no playmates and very little in the way of toys. For Christmas and on my birthday I was invariably given a doll. She always had bright blond curls, blue eyes, and white pale pink skin. These dolls were popular models of Shirley Temple, the famous child Hollywood movie star of the 1930s and 1940s.

Everyone made such a fuss over these dolls. "What beautiful blond curls . . . such gorgeous blue eyes," they'd exclaim, and ask, "Don't you wish you had such nice blond curls? Now you have a pretty doll to keep you company."

Whereupon I would gaze into my mirror and see my own straight brown hair and dark brown almond-shaped eyes. I concluded that I could never look like those revered dolls. Why didn't they think I was as pretty as the doll, I wondered, and my jealousy would turn to anger.

When I was forced to play with the dolls, I tore out their limbs or cut off their hair. More than once I remember tossing a brand-new doll out the window. They never lasted more than a few weeks.

Yet to my dismay I continued getting those dolls until the age of six, when I fell seriously ill and suffered a high fever. I remember vaguely how people knelt by my bedside and cried. Everything seemed bathed in a strange orange-and-pink light. Later I was told that I almost died.

When I recovered, my family presented me with yet another Shirley Temple doll. I cried and protested so loudly that they took away the doll and presented me with a wonderful stuffed rabbit. She was dressed in a plaid skirt and wore a red beret. I named her Joy, and she kept me company for many years. After that I got stuffed animals and no more dolls.

Four

The Magic of Pictures and Words

Without any toys I liked or books to capture my fancy, I would wander and explore the rooms of our flat as they spread out before me. Very often I'd search for interesting things to play with and usually got myself into trouble.

Once I took all the wooden clothespins from my mom's laundry basket, spread them out over a large blanket, and dipped each one in the jar of mustard. I emptied the leftover morning coffee into my mother's best crystal sherry glasses and stirred in lots of sugar.

Proud of my hotdog stand, I waited eagerly for my youngest brother, Georgie, to get home from school so we could play hotdog vendor.

I saw nothing wrong in what I did, and when my mom's screams were followed by blows from one of my dad's large leather belts, my bruised feelings hurt worse than the physical pain she inflicted.

I soon became aware that these sorts of creative deeds would get me into serious trouble. Nonetheless, I often went ahead anyway.

Another time, I cut up my mother's lace tablecloth and tied the pieces together with twine in order to make myself a party dress. I also removed the plastic flowers from the vase set in front of the holy picture of Jesus and formed them into a crown.

Standing before the mirror, I was almost breathless at the sight of my elegant self draped in white lace with a flowered tiara. Surely, I thought, my mother would be impressed with the splendid job I had done.

But again, I was given a repeated warning and a "good sound beating" by my mom.

It seemed that all my creative efforts were not getting me praise or rewards. Instead I was always in trouble and being spanked.

My aunt Maria often became withdrawn and could not always be counted on to watch me.

Soon my mother decided that she wanted me near enough so that she could keep an eye on me. My days of adventure and wandering alone through the empty rooms that had sparked my curiosity and creativity came to an end.

"You're as bad as my sons or worse," she scolded. "Four and a half years old, and instead of behaving like a little lady, you're just a tomboy!" I didn't know what behaving like a little lady was like, so I never felt very offended by that remark.

Undaunted in her effort to make a lady out of me, my mother decided to teach me how to embroider. My mother told me that when she was my age, she had loved sewing. She was sure she had found the right way to keep me occupied and set me up with my own little embroidery hoop that held a simple flower pattern. Then she threaded several large needles, each with a different color yarn, and showed me how to do a cross-stitch.

I sat there with my tiny thimble and tried to do as I was told.

Too often I stuck myself and complained. Finally, I just stitched every which way, ignoring the pattern. I found it all very boring.

My mother was to make another couple of attempts to teach me the art of the needle and thread. When I was about seven, she tried embroidery once more and failed. Still determined when I was about ten, my mother decided that I'd like crocheting. I ended up making a rather large knot about the size of an orange. Sewing, of any kind, has never appealed to me. To this day I cannot sew and hate having to hem a skirt or sew a button on a blouse.

Not pleased with my progress in embroidering, my mother decided I should spend more time in the kitchen. There I would help wash clothes in the large sink and assist my mother in preparing our meals. She'd give me little chores to do. She bought me a toy washboard and set me up on a wooden stool beside her as we washed dirty clothes.

Now and again as she worked, my mother would sing Puerto Rican folk songs. Her high soprano voice filled the kitchen with rich melodies. Sometimes the lyrics were playful and sometimes they were poetic and sad. I'd hum along and help pick out the discolored bits of rice or the tiny stones from the beans before she washed and cooked them. I'd grind down the spices with the wooden mortar and pestle for her.

But none of this helped me pass the time. Mostly I was unbearably bored. Yet if I complained, my mother would just find more dull work to give me.

In between jobs I'd find an excuse to get away from my

mom and searched around for something fun to do. One day my mother saw me trying to read the comics in the newspapers.

I asked her about the cartoon characters. "Mami, who are these funny-looking folks?" Then I pointed to the balloons over the characters' heads. I knew they were words and I wanted to know what they said.

Quickly, my mom got some scrap paper and a pencil and set me up in a corner at the end of the kitchen table. "Here," she said, "I want you to copy this picture. Like this . . ." My mom's repeated attempts to draw Dick Tracy lasted for about five drawings before she achieved a likeness.

Actually her final picture looked pretty good to me. She urged me to keep trying. "Now I want to see you do it, go on," she insisted.

By now I had become fascinated and started on my own attempt to draw Dick Tracy. To my surprise my first drawing wasn't bad. "That's very good," praised my mother. "Now do more. And here, do these others."

Upon hearing my mother's words of approval, I was eager to continue. This surely must be a ladylike thing to do, because it made my mother happy. And I wanted so very much to please her.

I showed her my next drawing of another comic character, Popeye the Sailor Man.

"Wonderful! What a smart daughter I have!" she shrieked. Now she wanted me to learn to draw all of them.

I had never before heard such praise from my mother for anything I had ever done. It made me very determined to impress her. That meant that I *had* to succeed. Every drawing had to be as good or better than the last one.

A line here, a circle there, another squiggle, mere lines could make all kinds of things happen on paper. I continued, totally captivated by all the magic that putting pencil to paper could accomplish.

As I worked diligently on my drawings, I realized that my mother's approval had come at long last. No longer was I a pest or unladylike. Perhaps because there was no such thing as television, and my mother could not find anything else for me to do, I began my career as an artist.

My mother had given me a sturdy cardboard box in which to keep all of my equipment. I treasured the pencils, crayons, and paper donated by my brothers. I continued to work with deliberate vigor on my drawings. My new work enriched my time, gave me a sense of accomplishment. And my mother's enthusiasm encouraged me to reach for greater challenges as I put images to paper. She was my best critic and gave me all of her support.

But whenever I asked her what the words meant, she would dismiss my questions and direct me back to the picture I was drawing.

Without understanding the circumstances, I somehow realized that my mother didn't know what the words meant. At that time I was not aware that my mother could not read or write in English. She only had the equivalent of a fourth-grade education and, in fact, had trouble reading and writing in her native language of Spanish.

My mother and I always communicated in Spanish. It was in the sweet sounds of Puerto Rican Spanish that my mother first spoke to me and sang her songs. Later, as an adult, I was able to appreciate my ability to speak Spanish. Beyond that, it is still a privilege for me to be able to immerse myself intimately and spiritually in my mother's culture.

At the same time that I was speaking only Spanish with my mother and my aunt, I also spoke English with my brothers. They talked among themselves mostly in English and so, to a large extent, I grew up bilingual.

Weekdays I waited eagerly for my brothers to come home from school. I loved to play with the youngest of my brothers, Georgie, who was going into the fourth grade. He was a great storyteller and would make up stories about haunted houses and ghosts, often scaring the rest of us.

Georgie and I also fought a lot, and I soon learned how to defend myself. If I complained too often, my mother would end up separating us. That was a punishment in itself, since it meant we couldn't continue our games. He taught me to play soldiers and cowboys and Indians.

When Georgie got too rough with me, the next older brother, Petie, came to my defense. Perhaps because he was two years older than Georgie, Petie was usually my protector.

In an effort to make me do more feminine things, my mother bought me a complete set of blue-and-white doll dishes. But Georgie wasn't interested in playing teatime, and at first the dishes remained in their gift box.

Then one day, quite unexpectedly, my brother Johnny came home from high school and asked if I would join him and bring my dishes. Then he asked me to set the table. He boiled milk in a small saucepan, stirred in sugar and a few drops of strong Spanish coffee, and poured the mixture into my toy teapot.

"Now we'll have a tea party!" he announced. I remember feeling so special and thrilled by the attention. After that and up until the time Johnny quit high school in his senior year and left home, I had a very exclusive and personal ritual with my oldest brother. We'd sit and chat. He'd ask how my day went. My brother would make a fuss about my recent drawings and always compliment my appearance. Johnny would also tell me about school and how well he did in baseball, his favorite sport.

My big brother created an awareness in me of what it meant to be a girl. Gradually my sensuous female instincts were gently awakened. Indeed, having my handsome, grown-up brother think that I was pretty and unique enhanced my existence. Before he got home from school, I would wash my face and hands, brush my hair, and tie a ribbon round my head.

I remember the thrill of waiting for him each afternoon. These rendezvous became my introduction to the power and charm of romance. It was also my big brother Johnny's generous gift to me.

My oldest brother eventually died tragically by his own hand, his death forever erasing any promise of a future. Still, those moments of sitting down with Johnny as he doted on my every word and drank from my tiny cup remain forever etched in my memory, just as tender and vivid as if it all happened yesterday.

As much as I enjoyed my drawing, I wanted to know what words all those letters formed. What were the words all these comic-strip characters were saying? When I asked my younger brothers, they became impatient with me. So I turned to my second-oldest brother, Vincent. Vincent was the serious one, the scholar of the family who maintained a straight-A average and expressed a thirst for knowledge.

Patiently, he set out to teach me to read. He printed each letter of the alphabet on a sheet of paper and had me copy each letter over and over until I got it right. He explained that words are made up of the twenty-six letters of the alphabet. "Once you learn these twenty-six letters, you'll be able to read and write all these words," he told me.

My mother had already taught me to count to ten by using my fingers. Now I began to learn not only the alphabet, but how to count up to twenty-six as well.

When everyone was home, it was not easy to find my own private space. My cousin Ralphy, who loved to build model airplanes, and my brothers seemed to take up most of the house.

My father often worked a night shift, and many times we all had to be quiet while he slept. That left our family with even less room in which to do our living. Everyone would have to create their own space. I would usually work on my bed.

Each day, I'd pick out a word printed inside the white balloons over a comic-strip character's head. Vincent would tell me what the word spelled. If the word spelled *happy*, he would instruct me to pick out the letters of the alphabet from the sheets of paper, place them in the right order, and then print the word.

I was a good student and worked hard on my lessons. In time I was able to pick out two or three words from the comics, then whole phrases.

As I progressed, I was thrilled when I realized that I could actually read words all by myself. I began to try to read the labels on milk bottles, cans of tomato sauce, and boxes of cereal. I tried to make sense of the headlines in the newspapers.

Sometimes Vincent would lose his patience when I followed him around, asking what a particular phrase or a word meant. "Stop following me!" he'd snap, exasperated by my persistence. Finally he'd threaten to stop teaching me another thing until I left him alone.

I would get back on Vincent's good side by drawing a picture of him working at his desk or reading a book. Then I'd print his name in large letters.

In fact, I began to find that drawing instead of just copying the comics was even more exciting. I was extremely curious about school and what my brothers did there. I knew they all came home with lots of books and notebooks.

When I'd ask Gilbert and Louie, who were my third- and fourth-oldest brothers, all about school, they each told different stories. My brother Louie would tell me all kinds of fibs.

"You have parties and they give you ice cream and candy—" he'd lie. "Cut it out," Gilbert would tell him. "You'll have her going to school expecting the wrong things." Gilbert told me that in school I would have to work hard, listen to my teacher, and be quiet and sit in my seat.

In my heart I wanted to believe Louie, but I also listened to Gilbert, who was the older of the two. In any case, I'd be finding out for myself because after the summer, I'd be attending kindergarten.

The very thought of school made me feel very grown-up. Besides, I mused, maybe Louie was telling the truth. Who knew what I might find in school? There were sure to be lots of great surprises.

These thoughts made me tingle all over with excitement.

Five
....

Summertime Freedom

*S*ummers were hot in the streets of *El Barrio* and even
hotter inside the tenements. There was only one little fan,
which sat on the kitchen window and blew in the hot night air.
But summer was also a season of fun and freedom for me,
because I was able to be outdoors a good deal of the time. School
was closed, and that meant that my brothers could baby-sit and
take me with them.

I remember my block in the summertime like a large stage,
with all the residents as the players in an ongoing play. Men set
up card tables and sat on makeshift chairs, stools, or wooden
boxes and played dominoes. Grown-ups sat on their stoop steps
or outside their buildings on folding chairs. Folks gathered
around Doña Josefina's candy store and the *bodega* to gossip and
discuss the economy and life in general.

The most talked-about subject for the adults was the war.
America had entered World War II in late 1941, and everyone
was excited and concerned. On some summer nights, air-raid
sirens sounded and everyone had to go indoors and turn off all
the lights. As soon as the sirens sounded again, everyone came
back out once more.

Many of the young men in the neighborhood had gone off to

fight; others were waiting to be drafted. There were war and defense posters displayed everywhere: in store windows, on buildings, on the sides of buses. Rallies were held to sell war bonds and raise money for the war.

My thoughts and concerns were not involved with a war that was being fought in a faraway place. Instead, my needs were closer to home, where I had to learn how to be streetwise, make friends, and stay out of trouble.

My brother Vincent bought me some chalk so I could draw on the sidewalk with the other children. In this way I could impress the kids with my cartoons and drawings of animals. It worked and I quickly made friends. Soon I learned how to play games with my new playmates.

The street had become my playground, and I was determined to make the most of it. I was almost five years old and out of my stroller. No longer a passive onlooker, I had now become one of the doers. I felt grown-up to be able to contribute to the ongoing events that created my neighborhood.

I enjoyed the freedom to make my own way through the throngs of people. I could choose to play, or to sit on the stoop while my brothers were busy playing stickball or just hanging out. They were always no more than a few yards away, keeping an eye out for me.

Whenever an adult turned on the fire hydrant, I followed the others and, with my clothes on, stepped into the ice-cold torrent of water. I'd stay under the spray long enough to drench my sweaty overheated self into a freezing shiver.

People screamed with exhilaration and clapped when the older boys pushed and carried the older girls into the cascading water. We all watched, amused, as the girls feigned resistance, then came out with their clothes soaking wet, squealing and giggling, and chasing the boys.

The street remained busy right up until nighttime. At dusk, after dinner, folks would come out again to enjoy the coolness of the evening. My mother and aunt joined some of the other women and did their mending or knitting. The men played their dominoes or gathered in groups, often having heated discussions about the war, politics, and sports.

The children played tag, or kick the can, hide-and-go-seek, follow the leader, or marbles, or we hung out near the teenagers until we were told to "get lost."

We lived only a few blocks away from Central Park. I remember that on Saturday nights when the weather was unbearably hot, my mother would pack a night picnic and we all went to the park. Often we were joined by neighbors.

My mom and dad would spread out some blankets, and I would run around the open meadow. I can still recall the sweet fragrance of the grass and the dampness of the earth under my feet, all so different from the world of concrete and asphalt a few streets away.

Petie and Georgie, Cousin Ralphy and I each brought along an empty jar with small holes punched into the lid. Then we set out to catch fireflies. We packed our jars full of fireflies and watched them flicker. It was fun to see all the other kids who had also filled their jars. The meadow looked like a parade of lanterns glowing in the dark.

I'd lie down on the grass and look up at the dark sky, watching the moon glide among the clouds and listening to the soft sounds of the crickets.

Some of the adults and kids speculated that we might be bombed by the enemy. "Bombs could fall from the sky and kill us all right now!" Cousin Ralphy told us. "It's scary when you think about it!" Everyone agreed.

I could not imagine being fearful when I looked at the miracle of a sky full of stars as they glistened against the deep blackness beyond.

My brother Gilbert told me that if I could find the largest star in the sky, I should make a wish and it would come true.

I remember searching for the largest stars and wishing on every one of them to let me and my family live in a place where I could gaze up at the heavens each and every night. I was convinced that if I could be free to see the stars, touch the cool earth, and bask in the soft sounds of summer, my personal connection with my own existence would be a happy one.

I had been to the movies before with the adults and remembered being mostly bored. But now I was able to go to the matinees with my brothers and share in their enthusiasm about the events up on the screen.

My mother would prepare a bag lunch and send us to spend almost the full day at the movies. We watched two double features, the serials, and lots of cartoons. I sat in a theater filled with screaming children and became fascinated by the images on the screen and intrigued by the plots and the words spoken by the actors.

The cartoons were easy to understand and so were the propaganda war movies. But what were all those grown-ups up there on the screen talking about in those other movies, I wondered. What was going on?

I pestered Petie and Georgie, asking so many questions that they often threatened to take me home. Sometimes they answered my questions and at other times I got poked and punched. Even Petie, who was normally on my side, would lose his patience.

"We're never taking you with us again, pest! Wait till I tell Mami how you acted!" But of course, they had to take me with them, and we all knew it. This was one of the few times where my mother could manage to have some time away from all of us, so I continued to ask questions.

Little by little I began to put things in order and soon began to understand the words and the plots. It didn't take long before I too was laughing and screaming just like all the others.

World War II was raging during 1943, and so were all the war movies. Our weekly movie matinees continued all summer long. And I saw American life as very different from the place I lived and from all the people I knew. On the screen, all the cowboys and war heroes were white Americans. Native Americans and Mexicans were the bad guys, Asians were war villains, blacks were servants and fools. The only white villains were the Nazis. All the stars and people who were important in the films were Caucasian. Many of them lived in private houses or in grand apartments.

I also figured that all of them must live in distant places

because when I left the movies and looked around for those people and their homes, they were nowhere to be seen.

I had experienced my first taste of freedom, to be able to play in the street and go to the movies. I was no longer confined (for the most part without playmates) in our apartment. I remember that leaving my passive existence, where I had felt restricted and overprotected, and stepping into an active childhood was absolutely invigorating.

I savored that first summer of freedom so much that to this day when summer arrives I feel like emancipation is moments away and that soon all my responsibilities will fade into thin air.

Of course, my responsibilities remain with me regardless of any season. But I still bask in that luxurious feeling of wonderment during the summer of my fifth year of life.

But summer came to an end, and everyone got ready for school. This time, instead of just watching, I got ready to go myself. I too was going to kindergarten. Kindergarten was a big word with lots of letters that meant it was most significant. I was quite impressed and felt myself to be very important indeed.

Six

....

Kindergarten

I had waited with anticipation for school and practiced all my letters and all my numbers. My brother Vincent had tutored me carefully so that now I could count to one hundred. I felt very proud and set out to show the teacher all I knew.

I was told to obey and listen to my teacher because I had been instructed that a teacher "is a very important individual." I was cautioned not to misbehave or speak out of turn.

"You must be a good girl and do exactly as you're told," my mother warned me. Otherwise, she promised, I'd have to answer to her and my father.

In class I sat at my desk like all the other children and looked with awe at my teacher. I don't remember her name, but I can still see her. She was a slender woman; now I can only guess her age to be her late forties. She had short gray hair, wore rimless glasses and a loose-fitting brown dress decorated with a white-and-green flower print.

Her manner was reserved and she seldom smiled. Occasionally she brought her index finger to her mouth and said, "Shhh . . . no talking. We must be quiet."

From time to time I checked out my classmates. Everyone had their hair neatly combed and sported new school clothes, just like me. My mother had brushed my hair till it shone. We sat with our hands clasped on our desks as instructed by our teacher.

Many details of that first day are a blur in my memory. However, the feeling of excitement that filled my being as I prepared to show the teacher that I could read lots of words and count way up to one hundred is still quite clear in my mind. I wanted to make her proud of me so that I could please her and please my family.

My reward would be teacher's praise.

The right moment arrived when I heard her ask the question, "How many of you here know how to count your numbers, and can anyone count to ten?" Immediately I raised my hand so high up in the air that I almost fell out of my seat.

Teacher asked me my name, and I told her. Then she asked me to count to ten. I stood and began counting. However, I didn't stop at ten. I kept on going until I reached about twenty-five. Then her loud voice commanded me to stop. But I announced to everyone quite proudly that I could count right up to one hundred.

"Is that so?" she responded. When she asked me to come up to the front of the class I honestly thought that she was going to allow me to finish counting up to one hundred. Instead she asked me to be quiet and face the students.

"Look at this show-off!" she said, digging her finger in between my shoulder blades. Teacher told the students hers was not a class for show-offs and continued reprimanding me. "When I ask you to do something, you do it. I said count to ten. I did not give you permission to count any further!"

All the children giggled and a few of them even pointed at me and made faces. After a few moments, she sent me back to my seat and promised to deal with me at another time.

I felt myself blush with shame. I was caught unawares and had no idea that I was doing something wrong. The humiliation brought tears to my eyes, but I swallowed and did not permit myself to cry. In order to cope with my feelings of disgrace, I simply withdrew. I would try never to be so bold again.

All my dreams of impressing the teacher and being rewarded for my hard work were dismissed in an instant.

Teacher took a dislike to me and for the rest of my kindergarten year, I was seldom called upon. When I bravely raised my hand, I was generally ignored. My attendance and behavior were satisfactory to fair. But my grades were always above average. I worked very hard on all my assignments even when I found the lessons boring.

My school was ethnically mixed with the children of immigrants: Italians, Irish, Eastern Europeans, and Greeks. There were also other Latino children, mostly Puerto Rican. A good percentage of the Puerto Rican children did not know English fluently. It was therefore natural for me to speak in Spanish to them. For this I was chastised and punished.

Once when a little girl did not understand the teacher, I forgot my resolution to stay passive and took it upon myself to raise my hand. When Teacher called upon me, I proceeded to translate in Spanish what the teacher meant to my classmate. Before my classmate could respond, Teacher yelled out her disapproval.

"We speak English in the United States of America," she

said, and told me that I was not in my old country. Then she addressed the whole class and told us that if everyone acted like me, no one would do any better than their parents. We would all be destined for failure. Where was our gratitude and our loyalty to America, she asked. Of course no one dared respond.

I was put in a corner facing the wall for the rest of the day. A corner which I remember well, with bare pea green walls, for I was sent there numerous times during the year.

I would sit on a chair facing the wall, looking for a discoloration in the paint, a crack in the plaster, or shadows on the surface. In this way I used my eyes and imagination to adjust these imperfections by making them take on other visual forms.

On that wall I remember a variety of scenes, among them trees and a waterfall, part of a schooner sinking at sea, and the profile of a horse. I was able to meditate upon these images and sit under the waterfall or walk in the woods.

Although I was still embarrassed and angry at Teacher, this game helped ease my punishment. At the same time, I enjoyed sharpening my sense of fantasy.

I also began to realize that I must never presume anything in front of Teacher. I must never let Teacher know that I could think for myself. Above all, I must never speak in Spanish, because this would certainly cause Teacher to become furious and punish me.

In class, I learned that it was dangerous to try to speak the language of my parents or my community. Nor was I ever to let Teacher see that I knew more than what she expected of me. As well, I should never introduce another way of doing things, even if, in my own judgment, it was a better way. Any kind of independent behavior meant that I could be publicly humiliated and punished.

At home I had been taught that as a matter of respect, when adults are addressing children, we must never look the adults directly in the eye. Children must out of deference lower their own eyes, listen, and answer with courtesy. When I did as I was taught, Teacher told me I was rude not to look at her. Such disrespect, she told me, would get me sent to the principal's office.

When I complained to my parents, they simply told me that the teacher was right. They were poor and had grown up in a colonized society, where going to school was a privilege reserved for the middle class and the rich. In their judgment school was sacred, and Teacher could do no wrong. They could not conceive of themselves as my ally in the face of such authority.

"You cannot contradict the teacher," my mother told me. She warned me that if she received just one complaint from school, I'd get spanked and be punished in a way that I'd live to regret. My father agreed. "Just do as you're told," he warned, "or you'll grow up to be a dummy."

These were not to be my only encounters with a school system that seemed to have no place for children like me. Indeed, my memories of school are often obscure, for when I begin to recollect, painful events at the hands of the school system come to mind.

Like so many poor kids, I had no other choice but to attend public school. I am convinced that had I not learned to read before I went to school, I might well have joined the ranks of those children of the poor who are ignored, put down by the school system, and never learn to read.

I learned to love books, became an artist and later on a writer, in spite of the New York City Board of Education's tutelage, not as a result of my public school education.

As a consequence of Teacher's rejection, I became more and more involved in my personal work at home. My mother gave me a small pair of scissors, and I began to do cutouts from cardboard. I used paste and colorful construction paper.

All of my treasures were well kept and organized in my "box of things," a wooden milk crate that contained and protected the contents that I created for the world of my imagination.

I made my own dolls out of cardboard and created pretty paper dresses for them. I made cardboard furniture, buildings, trees, flowers, and animals. In fact, I created a whole world for myself.

A world where I could be outdoors and where my people didn't fight and life did not cause us pain.

In my world only good things were possible.

Seven

....

Christmas Came with Joy and Plenty

*A*mong the many wonderful aspects of my Puerto Rican culture are poetry, storytelling, and music. Perhaps more than at any other time, during the Christmas holidays I experienced the richness of my ethnic background.

In celebration of the birth of Christ and the gifts of the magi, Christmas was a time of plenty. My mother and aunts called it *un milagro,* or God's mercy, because somehow money was found for gifts, a Christmas tree, and an abundance of food that we shared with our neighbors.

My parents and family would pool their funds and efforts and purchase a large pig from the local butcher. They would then carefully spice and prepare the pig in the traditional Puerto Rican manner. As soon as it was ready it was sent to an out-of-town bakery, which seemed so far away to us then. Actually, it was somewhere in the borough of Queens, adjacent to the borough of Manhattan where we lived.

The reason for this was that no one had an oven large enough to roast the pig. It was delivered to us hot and ready to serve on Christmas Eve, which was our night to celebrate. Traditional dishes like *arroz con gandules* (seasoned rice with dry green peas

42

and pork), *pasteles* (delicate meat pies made from root plants and plantains), and rice pudding were served.

Many of our neighbors also cooked this traditional feast, and the cooking aromas filled the entire tenement in which we lived. I thought the building would surely elevate to heaven just from the sheer goodness and delight of all those flavors floating and steaming in the atmosphere.

We got ready to party and greet our guests by piling the living-room furniture into the small bedrooms. All night long and into the early hours of the morning, friends and neighbors would come into our home, eat and visit. There was dancing, singing, and merrymaking.

It is part of our tradition, and therefore expected, that those who have food and drink open their doors and feed all who come to celebrate. People go from home to home, *parrandiando*. This is similar to caroling. *Parrandas* are groups of people who come to carouse on the Christmas holiday. Some are musicians, others poets and storytellers. They would play their guitars and employ a wonderful assortment of rhythm instruments as they sang the beautiful *aquinaldos,* Christmas songs praising Jesus and the miracle of the season.

Poets would recite traditional, as well as their own original, verses that spoke of their exquisite island where the gentle breezes and golden sun warmed one's soul. They spoke about their kinfolk far away, about loneliness, death, and isolation in a land where facing rejection and prejudice became a way of life. They lamented over the separation they endured, which was considered to be only temporary.

In their verses and in their stories, they were all going back someday, back to our *Borinquen, Isla del Encanto,* to our island of enchantment. Someday they would return, buy a good plot of land, and live off the generosity of the rich earth and the blessings of God. That seemed to be everyone's goal and the dream that gave our community hope.

During all the Christmas festivity I was allowed to stay up until I became too tired to stand. Then I was bedded down in one of the overcrowded rooms. Exhausted and happy, I slept soundly, oblivious to the noise and excitement in the other rooms. I was too busy dreaming of those special brand-new toys that might be waiting for me under the brightly lit, tinsel-trimmed Christmas tree.

Under the tree, I usually found some practical clothes, like a sweater or woolen knee socks, and (until I got my way) one of those dreaded Shirley Temple dolls. But I also found some blank drawing pads, construction paper, and large crayons.

For about a week and right up to January 6, *El Dia de los Reyes,* which is a big day of celebration in Puerto Rico, we ate Christmas food without worrying about asking for seconds.

Soon after, the Christmas tree was undressed and thrown out into the street and burned. I remember standing with my brothers as we watched the warm blaze illuminate the cold winter night.

Once more I was reminded of the reality of lean times, the daily monotony of school, and getting to bed early.

Many years have passed since those days of our family Christmas celebrations filled with sharing and cultural pride.

But I still remember how very moving and beautiful the lyrics of the songs were and the strength of the poetry recited. As each storyteller narrated a story with intrigue, or humor, or mystery, I sat listening, imagining and believing every word.

This early exposure to oral literature was, I am sure, a major reason that I was able to transfer easily from a career as an artist to a career as a writer almost overnight.

That rich cultural experience taught me to appreciate the beauty and power of language. It was also responsible for my love of books and my love of storytelling.

El cuento, el cuento puertorriqueno, storytelling was also used as a way to mollify any number of crises. When faced with tragedy or despair, any one of the adults might tell us not to worry because he or she was about to tell us a story.

Soon we were all enthralled, forgetting our grief, our hunger, or our anguish. When the story was over, our stress had lessened and once more life appeared endurable.

Eight
·········
Surprises, More Farewells, and Things Change

*M*y brother Johnny had already quit high school in his senior year and left home. My parents blamed it on the negative influence of his peers. "No-good guys," said my dad. "They don't want to work. Just steal and do drugs." But I remember that my oldest brother, for some reason or other, always argued with my parents, especially with my father. No one knew where he was. I remember the constant image of my mother praying before her altar, waiting and hoping to hear from her son.

My brother Vincent left college during his freshman year and joined the Army to fight in World War II. In a short time he made sergeant, and we were all so proud. I waited longingly for his letters and snapshots. I'd bring his picture to school, show off my handsome brother to the class, and feel very patriotic.

Our family had become smaller. My other four brothers and Cousin Ralphy were glad to have more space. But I missed Johnny and Vincent; they had always been there in my young life.

Now they were both gone.

I was at home the afternoon that Amy arrived. She was holding a suitcase with her coat draped over her arm, trying to hide her large stomach. My mother kept shooing me out of the kitchen so that I wouldn't hear their conversation. But I quietly snuck into the adjoining room and leaned against the wall so I wouldn't be noticed. I peeked in at them and listened intently.

She was Johnny's girlfriend, and she was pregnant. Amy told my mother that she had not seen Johnny in months but that she was almost eight months pregnant. Her mom had thrown her out when she found out that the father of the baby was Puerto Rican. Her family was of Ukrainian descent and quite prejudiced against anyone who wasn't white, she said.

Sobbing almost uncontrollably, Amy told my mother how much her mother hated Puerto Ricans. "She says my baby will be born black . . . that it will be a nigger and a spick." She had told her daughter to go find Johnny's people. If his family wouldn't take her, then her mother told Amy to live in the street. None of Amy's family would have anything to do with her now.

Amy told my mother how much she loved Johnny and wanted to be with him. She begged my mother to help her because she had no place else to go and no one to whom she could turn for help. "Please help me and my baby," she beseeched, and clung to my mother.

My mother stroked her gently and in a soothing voice told Amy not to worry, that she could stay with us as long as she wanted. Sooner or later, she was sure that Johnny would contact the family. But my mother promised to try through his friends to send Johnny news about the baby.

I had heard those words, "nigger" and "spick," yelled about in the playground at school, mostly by the older kids. I already knew my teacher did not respect me or my parents or the other Latino children in class. Now I heard that Amy's mother had told her to leave because Johnny was Puerto Rican. She didn't know us, yet she hated us because we were Johnny's family.

Standing in the darkness of the room listening to their conversation, a feeling of disorientation overwhelmed me. Why should people hate us so much? Were we really different? And if so, then in what way? Had I done something wrong? What had we done wrong? All of these questions made me slightly giddy.

Carefully I tiptoed to the other end of the apartment. I didn't want to hear any more. I wanted to forget all about people who hated us, and besides I didn't really understand why we were supposed to be so different. I took out some paper and began to draw a picture of Amy, with her big belly, and my brother Johnny. They were smiling and holding hands.

When Amy moved in with us, everyone had to be shifted around again and my brothers complained about having to surrender their newfound space. But I was glad to have another female in the house. She helped with the chores and proved to be no burden. My mother and aunt taught her to cook rice and beans and to say words in Spanish. Amy was bright and caught on quickly.

Despite my mother's efforts to contact Johnny, no one knew where he was. We found out that he was wanted by the police for hijacking and dealing in narcotics. But on the day Amy gave birth, he came to the hospital with flowers and candy. Before he disappeared once more, Johnny left Amy money and promised to come get her.

As soon as I saw baby Johnny, he stole my heart. He had lots of dark hair and the sweetest face. I held his tiny hands and measured his fingers against my own. They looked smaller than those of a doll.

I volunteered to feed and watch him. I tried to dress him and play with him. "He's not a doll to play with," my mother would tease me. "He's a real baby, you know."

I drew endless pictures of baby Johnny and became totally enamored of him. To me there was no baby more beautiful than my little nephew.

It was only later, as an adult when I had my own children—two boys—that I was able to feel that strong attachment and be so charmed by a baby once again.

From time to time, Johnny would send Amy a letter containing money but with no return address. Months passed and he never came to see Amy or the baby.

For the next six months, after school I would come home eager to see the baby and play with him. He began to recognize me and smiled reaching out for me. I sang to him and taught him to clap hands.

I had never had a younger sibling, and now I was able to form a strong bond with someone smaller and helpless. It made me feel important and grown-up to be an aunt at the age of six.

Then one day, when it was least expected, Johnny came in the middle of the afternoon. Amy packed all of their things and took the baby, and they drove away in Johnny's new car.

When I came home from school, baby Johnny was gone. There were no good-byes for me nor explanations of why they had left. I felt as if someone had taken the joy out of my life. For days and weeks I cried at night and thought about the baby every day. What was he doing right now? Does he miss me and will he forget me?

As the weeks passed, the memory of baby Johnny began to fade until one day I stopped thinking about him and went on with my life.

More changes were about to happen in our family. My parents felt that we needed a bigger apartment in a better neighborhood. "Better schools are in better neighborhoods," they reasoned. And so, before I knew it, we all moved again. This time our new apartment was another railroad flat a few blocks east of *El Barrio*.

White, ethnic families were the dominant group in our new neighborhood. They had their church, their food shops, and they owned most of the small businesses. We were the only Latinos living there.

Our family was typical of Puerto Rican families: one member looked Caucasian while another looked black, while others appeared as if they could cross over into either race.

In those days there was no such group as "people of color." You were either Caucasian, or Negro, or Oriental.

Today I am most grateful that Latinos and African-Americans are designated as "Americans of color" because this grouping does not force us to choose sides. But back then we were conspicuous in *that* racially homogeneous surrounding, and unwelcome. I remember the name-calling and our mailbox being ripped open and our correspondence destroyed. Human feces was left at our doorstep, and once we opened a parcel to find a dead rat inside.

My first attempt to play with the children was quite successful. The kids were friendly and even asked if I could visit with them. But when I went down a second time, the grown-ups interfered. They had obviously prepared their children to hate and to attack me, for I was verbally and physically abused in the presence of the adults who joined in the name-calling.

"Go back to where you came from, spick!" was followed by a slap from one of my young playmates while another spat on me. "You're nothing but a bunch of niggers," yelled a woman, followed by shouts from everyone. "Go live with your own kind!"

I remember being afraid to leave the house and became terrified of just walking down the street. Two of my brothers were brutally beaten; one had both eyes blackened and the other suffered a fractured shoulder. My father was also attacked on the way home from working a night shift and had to have a large number of stitches to close a gash across his head and forehead.

The white priest in the all-white parish informed my mother that there was nothing he could do. In fact, he told us that it might well be our family that was causing problems because there were all good people in the neighborhood. Perhaps it was our family who wasn't comfortable, and he went so far as to suggest that we might be better off living in a neighborhood with people who understood us and our ways.

My brothers wanted to go back to our old neighborhood and bring some friends in order to strike back. "They want to fight, we'll show them what Puerto Ricans can do," threatened my brother Gilbert. But my mother and aunt were terrified that one of us might be killed, and they put a stop to any talk of warfare.

After lots of arguments and family discussions, my brothers, Cousin Ralphy and I, and my aunt, all gave a sigh of relief when my parents decided to move. Our attempt at living in an all-white area had lasted approximately four months.

We went to live on Prospect Avenue in the South Bronx, where the majority of the people were Puerto Ricans who shared their working-class neighborhood with the immigrant families of Italians, Greeks, Irish, and a sprinkling of Jews.

That experience—when in my young life I witnessed hatred, abuse, brutality, and xenophobia based solely on the fact that we were Puerto Ricans—will remain with me for the rest of my life.

In fact, my novel for young readers titled *Felita* was based upon this incident in my life.

*A six-year-old with all the world
before her.*

When World War II broke out, my brother George joined the Navy . . .

and my brother Vincent, the Army.

Aunt Maria
with Johnny,
my older brother
Johnny's son.

Here's my brother
Gilbert in a high
school photo.

And here I am, age thirteen,
all dressed up for a school recital.

My special pal Sporty. Here he is on the roof of our apartment on Prospect Avenue in the Bronx, despite the warning.

On Prospect Avenue in the Bronx. In the 1950s you could hang out, take in a movie, have a soda, show off your bike, like my brother Pete.

My mother, Nicolasa Rivera,
in a photo taken around 1947.

Graduation from junior high school. Mom made the dress and fancy hair ribbon. My family supplied the flowers.

*The years passed.
I was a senior
in high school
when this picture
was taken.*

*Today, in my
study at home,
working on my
next project.*
(Photo by Phil Cantor)

Nine
· · · · · · · ·
Freedom to Learn
and Reflections on Religion

*O*ne of the most thrilling events I can recall was when I got my first library card. I was seven and a half years old. My brother Vincent was home from the Army after the war and decided it was time for me to choose my own books.

I had never been in such a place, where books were everywhere, on shelves that reached up to the ceiling, on tables and pushcarts. Vincent helped me fill out my application, and I received my library card that very same day. After looking at several books, I decided to take home *Pinocchio* by Collodi. I was mesmerized by the illustrations and stimulated by the story.

Vincent helped me read the words I could not understand. I borrowed this book at least three times, until the librarian told me I should try another book. "Why not try Grimm's fairy tales?" she suggested, and assured me that I could still take out *Pinocchio* whenever I wanted.

I went on to read many books dealing with fairy tales and fables. As I got older I began to read adventure stories, including those by Jack London, Mark Twain, and James Fenimore Cooper. I also read the mysteries of Agatha Christie and all the Nancy Drew, Horatio Alger, and Pollyanna books. Reading became an avenue of freedom compared to the boring textbooks

61

and the restrictive reading program that was offered to me in school.

One of the many kind librarians who took an interest in me and my love of books introduced me to the works of Howard Fast. I read about young Tom Paine and at that point became interested in history and decided that there were many books that I had yet to discover and to read.

Yet as I read book after book, there remained in me a sense of dissatisfaction. No matter how many books I read, I never saw myself in any of the stories. I never saw *my* family. No author spoke to *me* about the value of who *I* was as an Hispanic American child. I was invisible in North American literature. I did not exist, and my family and community did not exist either.

I had no knowledge of Spanish or Latin American literature. Even if I did I still could not have read these books because I did not know how to read in Spanish.

Spanish as spoken by the Puerto Rican population was the language of my emotional life, the language I heard at home and within my own community. But outside my home and neighborhood, English was ubiquitous. It was the language that commanded; it was the language of the greater society out there. And I understood early on that English was my language of survival. In order to succeed I had to excel in English.

Despite these considerations, when I got to junior high school I quickly decided to take Spanish as my second language. This decision proved to be a damaging experience. Our teacher, an Anglo-American, taught only Castilian Spanish. She was constantly correcting, humiliating, and embarrassing all the Latino children who could not speak with the Castilian lisp. "You speak like a bunch of Chinamen," she criticized, and informed us that Puerto Ricans spoke Spanish incorrectly.

After the year was up, I switched my language to French and never again attempted to learn Spanish in school. It was much later on, during my trips to Puerto Rico and when I studied art in Mexico, that I began to read and understand a more sophisticated and scholarly Spanish.

I wonder how my junior high Spanish teacher would have felt if someone had forced her to speak English like the British upper classes, and humiliated her by demeaning her thick Irish-American Bronx accent. But children do not have the power to demand justice, and so I did the next best thing: I made sure this teacher was out of my life.

My access to the New York Public Library was what allowed me to pursue my thirst for knowledge. It was there that I sought out an education for myself. The library was a long walk from home, and I was not allowed to go by myself. But I took every opportunity to have my brothers or an adult take me there. Sometimes I persuaded them to let me stay longer and pick me up later on their way home.

I'd sit and read, do my homework or browse through the many wonderful books that lined the shelves. The librarians were friendly and helpful. It was quiet, and that made it easy to concentrate.

Now I did not have to withdraw into a world of inner silence in order to think. By going to the library I had the choice to get away and do my work in peace. It was my refuge, a place away from the crowds and the clamor, away from my crowded apartment. The library became my home away from home.

I couldn't wait to be able to take books out of the grown-up section one day. And in time I did just that.

Libraries are sometimes called colleges for the poor. Indeed, this was true in my case. I continued to use the library as a place where I could do my schoolwork or simply sit and think without noise or distraction. To this day I continue to use the library.

At the age of fourteen, I got my working papers and got my first job as a page girl in the public library. I sorted books, filed cards, and assisted the librarians with any number of chores. I held this position right up to my high school graduation when I was seventeen years old.

I've often thought that had I not become an artist and a writer, I might very well have found my calling as a librarian. A noble profession as keeper of the books.

As thrilling as getting my library card was, making my first communion was an unhappy experience.

I never attended Catholic school, mainly because we couldn't afford the fee. But even if that had not been the case, I know my father would have refused to pay for it. We were all well aware of his disdain for organized religion and understood that he would never agree to send any of his children to Catholic school. Therefore, I went to catechism twice a week instead.

If there is any one area where my father had a significant influence on my development, it was in the areas of religion and politics. We never really interacted much, and he was not affectionate toward me. But in this instance, he would sit me down and try to explain the principles of socialism and communism. Several times, without my mother's knowledge, he took me to closed meetings with guarded doorways, where visitors had to be members. There people, mostly men, made speeches about equal rights and religion as the opium of the masses.

"Don't be superstitious or foolish like your mother," Papa warned me. He told me to question everything I was told at religious instruction. Papa informed me that it was the dominant society and the bosses that wanted all of us to be docile and believe in God. This way we would always obey the ruling classes and never fight for justice. It was the church's way, and the way of capitalism, to make sure the working class would do their bidding.

When I asked him if he believed in God, he'd snap right back at me. "There is no God. There is humanity and only the here and now. Forget about heaven and hell. Heaven and hell are right here on earth. Heaven for those who have, and hell for those who haven't."

I remember slogans like "Equal work means equal pay" and "Fight for your union" or "Down with capitalism" and "Power to the people."

I would never have acquired these audacious views from my mother. If he has given me nothing else, I've always been grateful for my father's interest in making me see another side. Otherwise, I truly believe that I would have grown up much more willing to accept authority figures and their ideas at face value without really questioning their truth or purpose.

Most of what was said at those meetings went over my head. The diatribes barely held my interest. What I enjoyed the best was the free soda and snacks served after each meeting. But my father had set me thinking, and I wondered about the ideas we dealt with during catechism and what they really meant. Consequently, I wondered about what the nuns told me and I questioned the idea of confession itself. If there was a God, and if he heard everything and was everywhere, then why couldn't I talk directly to Him?

I used to hear my own mother praying at night. She spoke to God directly and recited prayers given to her at *El Centro de Espiritismo.* Once when I questioned my mother about these prayers, she told me that they were said for distinct reasons according to one's individual needs and that I was not to bother the nuns about it.

But one day I told the nuns about my mother's altar and about some of our visits to the *Centro,* where they played drums, rattled necklaces, danced, and went into trances. The sisters became quite upset and told me that my mother was committing a sin. "If this is true," they told me, "then have your mother come in and talk to us."

When I told my mother about how distressed the sisters were and how she had to come in to see them, she merely shook her head and lightly chided me. "Silly, why did you have to upset the sisters?"

Then she explained that her prayers and the *Centro* had nothing to do with the nuns. This was personal and outside the realm of nuns or priests; this was *ours.* My mother told me that our way of worshiping was as important, powerful, and spiritual as the laws of the Vatican itself. People had been worshiping in this way since our ancestors had come from Africa and fused cultures with the indigenous Tainos of the island and Roman Catholicism. It was not for the Catholic Church or any government, she asserted, to define our spiritual beliefs. Then she instructed me never to discuss it with the sisters ever again.

My mother's response both surprised and reassured me. It seemed when her spiritual beliefs were threatened, she affirmed her authority. My mother's reaction and attitude let me know that our religious convictions had value and that our culture was to be respected.

As I got older, my mother got more frantic that I should conform and honor my religious obligations. I overheard her telling my aunt that I had to make my communion and confirmation before I became *una señorita.*

She did have good reason to worry. During those afternoons when I was scheduled to go on to religious instructions, I'd leave school, stay outdoors, and play. The result was that I never passed my religious tests and was not ready to make my communion.

I had just turned eleven years old and most of the kids I knew had already made their communion and confirmation. Finally, my mother pleaded with the only Spanish priest in our parish. He agreed to overlook my transgressions and pass me anyway. Much to my disappointment, I was given a date and expected to behave and go to confession, make my communion, and subsequently be confirmed.

Now, I truly dreaded going to confession and I had my good reasons. Just the previous year, I had gone to an early Sunday mass on purpose with my friends. We knew that the grown-ups would not be attending. I was there on a dare to go right up to the altar and take the wafer. Of course, I still had not gone through my communion or confirmation or even gone to confession, and my action was considered a sin. But I was determined to show my friends that I didn't care.

When I found myself in church sitting in a pew that morning, I could hardly keep from trembling. My breakfast (which I was supposed to skip when taking the wafer) lay in my gut like a load of lead.

My friends were all smiling and others were jeering. Finally I heard one of them say, "You gonna go or are you scared?" I stood up and went right up to the altar and waited, forgetting everything my father said about there being no God. I kneeled and closed my eyes, resigned that I might be struck dead at any second. I peeked out my right eye and saw the priest getting closer and closer as he distributed the communion wafer. I shut my eyes tightly and opened my mouth like everyone else until I felt something as thin as paper being placed on my tongue. I opened my eyes and closed my mouth. The thin wafer was tasteless and melted in my mouth.

"Now you'll go to hell for sure," said one of my playmates. But I found myself alive and still standing. I had not been struck dead or even found out. So I turned around with great confidence and said, "That's only your opinion."

When the time came for my confession, I never told the priest about my trip to the altar. I also neglected to confess about how I often took candles and lit them without putting money in the box. I enjoyed watching the candlelight glow in the darkness of the church and the smell of melting wax. I'd glance up at the statues and wonder if they could move. I was very careful not to stare directly at them or linger too long; after all, I couldn't imagine the saints approving of my behavior.

Anyone who heard my confession would have believed I was the model child. According to me I never lied or swore, never took anything, and never had impure thoughts. I did not quite know what "impure thoughts" meant. But I knew I was not admitting to any of them anyway.

The day after my first confession I put on the beautiful white dress with a veil and a matching handbag that my mother and aunt had made for me. I wore white stockings and white shoes. Most of the kids were at least three years younger than me, and I felt awkward and out of place. I marched along, trying not to sulk. "Today we are supposed to be marrying God," a little girl told me. Well, I thought, since Papa says He doesn't exist, it can't be a real marriage.

In the years that followed I went to confession as little as possible. I confessed only a fraction of my childhood transgressions and never completed reciting the prescribed penance. By the time I was thirteen, I decided that I would attend church on Sundays (as was expected of me), but I would no longer go to confession.

Today, although I do not adhere to any particular secular religious group, I have an affinity for the spiritual beliefs that were brought into the Caribbean by our African ancestors.

Ten

....

Deaths in the Family

While I was dealing with my own life, my father had been suffering from a heart condition. During his last stay in the hospital, he died. He had gotten quite ill and although his death was expected, it was a terrible blow. My mom was especially stricken since she had not been well herself.

"How are we going to manage?" she cried over and over. Now, upon reflection, I realize that she was right to worry, because harder times did lie ahead.

My father had been a merchant seaman, and later an unskilled laborer. When he died, he had nothing to bequeath us. In spite of all his years of work for the unions and his devotion to socialism, there was no pension or fund set aside for his widow and children. My mother had to use every bit of his life insurance on a modest funeral.

I was intrigued by death. Death. What did it really mean? It meant that we would never see Papa again, my brothers informed me. Never again. Death is for ever and ever, my aunt Maria told me, and it can't be undone.

I remembered a little boy named Raymond, who got hit by a truck and was killed. He was about six or seven. They had held his funeral in an empty store. People filed past his little coffin and looked down on Raymond dressed in his Sunday best with a white communion armband on his sleeve. I hardly recognized him all dressed up like that, with his pink cheeks and hair neatly combed. I recollect questioning whether the dead boy was really Raymond. "Sure it's Raymond, you dummy!" my brother Georgie assured me. "You'll never see him again. He's dead!"

The loss of my father had been my very first intimate encounter with the consequences of a death. I loved my father, but he was much older than my mother, and I often felt like he was more of a benign grandfather figure. He was never mean to me, nor did he ever spank me. But there was not that intimate bond that I had established with Martin. He showed no interest in my drawings or in any of my childish games. Except for his concern over politics, my father showed very little interest in the things I did. Most significant for me was that he never celebrated my existence.

Everyone at home was devastated and mournful. I wanted to feel a great loss just as the rest of my family, but instead my own feelings of sorrow were disconnected.

Then, a few weeks after my father was buried, I found a dead sparrow while playing in an empty lot. I saved the little bird behind some bricks. I went and got an empty wooden matchbox, decorated it with construction paper and colored it with crayons, and placed one of my hankies on the inside as a lining. I took two twigs, tied them together with yarn, and made a small cross. The box was a trifle small. I had to work carefully to squeeze and fold the dead bird, who was quite stiff by now, until it was all stuffed inside the box.

I had made two friends, Alberto and Marilyn, and invited

them along for the burial ceremony. Since I had already gone through the ritual of holy communion and confirmation, I knew my prayers and recited one of Our Father and two Hail Marys for the soul of the departed sparrow.

Alberto was Pentecostal, and he sang a song in Spanish praising Jesus and asking him for mercy for the departed. Marilyn was Jewish, and she penciled the Star of David on the box and also said a prayer for the dead in Hebrew. Then we dug out a hole in the abandoned lot, behind a wall where the grave would be safe, and we buried the sparrow. We assured ourselves that after such a pious ceremony, the little bird would surely go up to heaven.

That night in my bed, I remembered the dead sparrow and his cold lifeless body as it lay in the palm of my hand. I had buried it into the ground exactly as they had buried my father. I imagined how the sparrow would never fly again or sing again. I was grief-stricken and felt a deep loss for the dead bird.

By personally performing a ritual for the dead sparrow and lamenting its demise, I was finally able to mourn for my father. I used the sparrow as a symbol in order to connect with the reality of death. Somehow the ceremony and burial of the bird was the bridge that allowed me to imagine and grasp the death of my father. For the first time since my father had died, I began to cry in earnest. It was only then that I understood that I would never again see Papa sitting on his favorite chair, reading his copy of the *Daily Worker*. He would no longer sit at our table or take us to the park on Sundays.

"Papa's gone . . ." I cried, and was able to mourn and accept the loss.

• • •

The Bronx is where I blossomed into womanhood, where I sustained great disappointments and overcame tragedies. I remember our large apartment on Prospect Avenue was always filled with people. It was the grandest apartment we had ever occupied. It had five bedrooms, a kitchen, and, although it still had only one bathroom, it was bright and had spacious rooms with lots of windows. All the rooms extended off a long foyer, and we had a front and a back view with an elongated fire escape.

At first, we were all happy to have so much room, but my mother was always providing shelter for a needy relative or friend, so living space continued to be scant. My very own room was mostly temporary. My mother would explain to me how we had to help out our cousins, or this poor woman and her son, etc., because they had no one else to turn to. With reluctance I'd move back into my mother's room.

Then one day, two years after my father had died, we received news from an old friend who was in deep trouble. It was Martin. He was very sick and was suffering with lung cancer. Most of his life he had smoked two to three packs of cigarettes daily. He also drank excessively. When I was told that he was coming to stay with us, I was overjoyed. Secretly, I hoped he would take my father's place.

I fantasized that Martin would get well and take care of us. I would call him Papi, and it would be all right then. Because he would be legally married to my mother, I could even use his last name. We would have no bad worries once Martin became the new head of our household. But my joy was short-lived and my fantasy quickly shattered. Martin had been operated on for lung cancer and sewn back up again. There was no hope of a cure. My mother, who was a generous and compassionate person by nature, had agreed to let Martin live his remaining days with us.

"His brothers and sisters have no use for him," she explained to me, "and he has no one but us." I was to see a side of Martin that upset and disturbed me. He was in a great deal of pain, and at first my mother did not want to limit his drinking. "It seems to ease his pain," she told us, "so what is the harm in that?"

But during these drinking sprees, Martin became verbally abusive and had temper tantrums. Often he'd smash a glass or piece of furniture and bang his fists against the wall. I remember the blood oozing down his arms. Ultimately, my mother had to threaten to throw him out if he didn't stop drinking.

Instead of becoming closer to Martin, I began to resent him. I was too old for the nonsensical games little children enjoy and too young to understand his pain and desolation. Finally, he became so ill and went to the hospital, never to return.

I needed no symbol to mourn Martin. I remembered our time together. The stories he told me, the card games I always won, his special dinners made just for me, the six-legged chicken, and the way he doted on my every word and praised everything I did. I remembered his unconditional love and wondered about this man. The veracity of my birth haunted me still.

Red had been Martin's favorite color, so I took the few cents I had saved and bought him some red socks. Then I drew a picture of Martin smiling, healthy, and happy, as I had once known him. My mother agreed that although the socks did not match the dark suit in which he was to be buried, she would make sure he wore them. She would include my drawing as well.

I wept with anguish at Martin's funeral and deeply regretted that he and I had not been able to recapture that magic we had once shared nor the love and closeness that had bonded us when I was a very little girl.

The difficult questions I never asked Martin invade my thoughts now and again. If indeed he was my biological father, the possibility of a relationship between daughter and father had vanished. That tender possibility of what might have been and the memories of his charm have stayed with me all of my life.

Eleven
....
A Teacher Cares

School was better in The Bronx. There were fewer students in a classroom, and the corridors were not as noisy as my old school. But things remained more or less the same for me until I reached sixth grade. Finally, I encountered one of the few good teachers of my school experience.

Mr. Johnson was a tall person with a head of unruly straw-colored hair. I was becoming more and more bored with school. After the deaths of Papa and Martin, and given the pressures created by changes at home, I became withdrawn and petulant in class and refused to participate in any discussions.

One day, Mr. Johnson had a discussion on special talents and our future. One kid played the clarinet, another played the piano; both were considering musical careers. A black girl said she wanted to become a great singer like Marian Anderson. There was also a boy who liked to draw. I had seen his work and he was not as good as I was, probably because he didn't practice as much as I did. Mr. Johnson said that he knew there were two artists in class and called upon both of us. The boy said he wanted to be a cartoonist. I said I wanted to be an artist who could draw everything in this world and have my work shown in museums.

As soon as I spoke, Mr. Johnson challenged me by asking me to draw something on the blackboard. Suddenly I felt stupid, as if everybody was staring at me, and I didn't move. "That's because she can't really draw good," said the boy who wanted to be a cartoonist.

My training, as a member of a large family and the only girl, was to stand up to a provocation, especially when the dare dealt with familiar ground. Now I was determined to show him and the class what I could do. I walked up to the blackboard with total confidence.

I asked Mr. Johnson if he had a special request. Anything I wanted to draw would do, he said. But just then the boy yelled out and dared me to draw a ship with pirates because girls could only draw dolls and baby animals. Everyone laughed, but the teacher said that I was to draw only what *I* wanted. I remained confident, because a ship and pirates doing battle was a favorite scene among the many that I had carefully copied out of adventure books.

I picked up the chalk and carefully drew the bottom of the ship, then the sails and the cannons and, to top it off, a pirate flag with skull and crossbones, followed by the water and clouds. Then I began drawing figures of pirates with swords and guns. I could hear the *oohs* and *aahs* from the class, and this fired me on. I drew another ship in the distance on the attack.

After my demonstration, I enjoyed the attention and admiration I received. Even my antagonist challenger had to admit I could "really draw."

From the very beginning when I put pencil to paper, I recognized my ability to draw as an asset at home, in the street, and in school. This special talent set me apart from most of the other children and gave me an edge, a place from which I was allowed to excel.

Even the most narrow-minded and prejudiced teachers were impressed by my ability. I remember a teacher in third grade who was a frightful bigot. She would not even tolerate a greeting in Spanish between pupils. She'd lecture to us on the virtues of being real Americans and say things like, "Why don't you folks try to speak like Americans?" or "You're all too ungrateful to be allowed in this country." In spite of her low expectations of Latino children, I once overheard this same teacher talking to a colleague about me. "Nicholasa has talent, so she can't be all bad," she remarked.

Mr. Johnson encouraged me to draw posters for the school library for the celebration of Washington's and Lincoln's birthdays. He had me design sets for a class play about Pilgrims landing on Plymouth Rock for Thanksgiving. He told me that I was smart and should definitely go on to college and earn a degree in fine arts. I had only had him for a semester and a quarter when, much to my discouragement, he was transferred to another school. Yet he was one of only two teachers who did their best to help me. The other was an English teacher in high school.

Sadly I can remember no one else caring or helping me during my New York City public school experience.

Twelve

············

A Social Worker's Wrath and Mother's Fortitude

$\mathcal{B}$y the time I was twelve, our family had changed. We were no longer all together. My brother Johnny was in an out-of-state prison for drug dealing and drug use. Vincent was married and lived in Connecticut. Gilbert had joined the Army and gotten married. Louie had also joined the Army and had been sent overseas. My cousin Ralphy was in the Marines and stationed at one of their bases down South. Louie sent us a small allowance and my married brothers helped out when they could, since they now had their own responsibilities. Ralphy sent an allowance to Aunt Maria.

My mother had become the head of our household. In a way, my mother's status as a widow seemed to set her free and make her more independent. She had always been a strong person, decisive in dealing with her family. Now she was in charge of keeping the household together and had to furnish us with food and shelter. She was uneducated and possessed no particular skills that were valuable in the job market, yet somehow she managed to provide for our needs.

Even when my father was alive, we had always been poor and lived from paycheck to paycheck. My dad made sure we had food on the table, clothes for school, and a roof over our heads.

Anything beyond these essentials, such as extra clothing, toys, or eating out, would have been considered luxuries. Except for a holiday or a birthday celebration now and again, there was never extra money for any of those things.

In the days that followed my father's death, however, finding money for our basic needs became a problem. Our daily life was conditioned by financial insecurity. My mother received some public assistance and was able to find work at the small sewing factories known as sweatshops. She made very little money and did not want to jeopardize the few dollars we received from public assistance. My mother was clever and a good worker and convinced the bosses to pay her off the books.

Nonetheless, we depended on the goodwill and approval of the social workers who invaded our home and our lives. We had many instances where they insisted on searching our apartment to see if we had bought anything new. Caseworkers were also looking for unlisted live-in relatives, boarders, or a father who was declared missing but who might actually be hiding in a back room.

Sometimes a caseworker would try to interrogate me and my brothers to see if there was any extra money coming into the house. We always knew how to behave. We were very polite, said nothing, and knew even less. It was all part of our family's survival.

Things usually went along smoothly, but there was one time that such a visit just about devastated me.

My mother had accepted a new member into our household. He was a fluffy-haired puppy, medium to small, white with black and tan markings. A relative had asked us to care for him for only a few weeks. My mother loved animals and could not refuse. In fact, we now had a cat that my mother named Miss-meow and her beloved canaries, Pepito, Raul, and Reina. My mother loved her three birds. They were given to her by a relative who was in the merchant marines and brought them to her as a present. She would sing to the birds, and had trained them to sit on her hand and eat from her lips. She was vigilant in keeping Missmeow away from her birds, and the cat knew better than to go near them. Somehow all the animals managed to live together quite well. My mother was like a child in her love for animals.

Much to my delight, our relative forgot about his dog. Everyone liked Sporty, who was friendly and smart. Although he became the family pet, Sporty was really my dog and everyone knew it. I'd feed and walk him. After school I'd run home, where Sporty was eagerly waiting for his walk. I'd leash him and we'd rush out to play. At the school playground I'd show off how smart my dog was. I'd get Sporty to shake hands, beg, roll over and play dead. Sporty was quite a ham and loved to impress the kids, so he was popular with everyone.

I loved the way he'd put his head on my lap, sigh, and look up at me with his sweet brown eyes. At night when my mother was asleep I'd sneak him into my bed, though there would be hell to pay. My mom would complain about hair all over my bedding and the way I smelled of dog. But in time my mother relented and let Sporty sleep by my side.

Once there was a false fire alarm because Mrs. Alvarez who lived on the second floor of our building forgot to turn off the stove burner and her pot of beans burned. Black smoke was everywhere and we had to evacuate the building. I thought only of saving Sporty, so I grabbed him and fled. My mother, unaware that I was out of the building, began crying out for me.

Afterward, my mother became furious because I had thought about the dog first instead of my family. It was only an animal and not human, she reminded me. Still, she had taken her birds and made sure the cat was safe, so she was hardly convincing. When I told her that I didn't care and still loved Sporty best, she shook her head. But I discerned a smile on her face.

One year we were lucky enough to have a social worker who didn't mind our having pets. She was a gracious person who always accepted *un cafe con leche* and chatted with my mom. One day she was taken ill with an emergency appendectomy, and another social worker was sent in her place.

The new social worker refused my mother's coffee. Her demeanor was intrusive and rude. She became irate because we were keeping pets. "Our money is not for you people to have pets and other luxuries," she rebuked us. If we wanted these things, she told us, we should go out and work for them like hard-working Americans did. She even threatened to report us and stop our checks.

My mother tearfully pleaded with her and denied that any of these animals belonged to us. She told the woman that Sporty belonged to a neighbor and that the dog would never be allowed in our house again. The birds belonged to her sister who was on vacation, and she was coming to take them back tomorrow. As for the cat, it was a neighborhood cat that was a good mouser. Since we had a mouse problem she let it in once in a while.

Actually, it really wasn't anyone's cat, my mother assured the social worker.

I was mortified to see my mother humiliated in this way and became distressed at the thought of having to give up my dog. I remember going into the kitchen with Sporty on his leash and quietly sobbing.

Fortunately, my mother had no intention of giving up Sporty or any of our animals. She devised a plan to hide Sporty, Missmeow, and her birds with our neighbors. We would simply clear away their bowls and cages when it was time for the caseworker's next visit. "I won't let them take Sporty or any of our animals," she reassured me. "Don't worry. They are part of our family and we must all be together."

And we did just that for about two months. It was quite a routine. One neighbor got Sporty, another Missmeow. My mother sent Pepito, Raul, and Reina to stay with Doña Laura, an elderly woman who lived with her unmarried daughter. My mom made sure that her birds would be in a quiet environment. "I don't want my birds upset by kids poking at them," she told me.

Our old social worker recuperated and was back on our case. The dreaded caseworker visits became pleasant once more.

My mother taught me that to love another species was nothing to be ashamed of, because we are all creatures of nature loved by God. It is one of the many precious things she gave me from her treasure chest of human values.

Thirteen

Making Up and Shedding Enemies

$\mathcal{M}$ost of the kids in my neighborhood also went to my junior high school. But after the burial ceremony of the sparrow, Alberto and Marilyn had become my two best friends. They were also classmates.

I liked my school and had made friends. I had become used to being with girls, and I liked the bonding we achieved. I had spent so many years with males, listening to sports events and male chatter. Now I began to appreciate how much I could share with members of my own sex. We went window-shopping on Prospect Avenue, talked about clothes and about how silly boys could be.

Even though I was getting older, I still hung out with Alberto. He had few friends outside his church community, and I felt a little sorry for him. His parents were Pentecostal fundamentalists and very strict. They forbade their son to associate with other children who were not church members. Since I used to attend services once in a while, his parents accepted me.

I enjoyed their Pentecostal services, especially their lively music. A heavyset blond woman would play a large old black piano accompanied by two guitar players and a percussionist who played some mean drums, timbales, and bongos. When they played religious music the whole congregation jumped and shook until no one remained seated.

People confessed the most outlandish sins out loud, for everyone to hear. They asked for forgiveness for their marital infidelities, acts of prostitution and criminal activities, and all sorts of sins against their church. I found the whole event absolutely amazing.

This was a far departure from the secret confessions and the boring Catholic mass performed in Latin in my own church. I remember trying to stifle my yawns as I listened to the priest deliver a colorless sermon, usually on sin, responsibility, and guilt.

Marilyn's parents owned a dairy store in the neighborhood where they sold milk, cheese, and eggs. Their apartment was in the back of the store. Sometimes her dad would give me a half-dozen eggs that were cracked or an assortment of unsold cheeses to bring home. My mother would pass by to thank them and return their generosity by giving them some of her fresh cut chamomile or sage.

Every day after regular school, Marilyn attended Hebrew school. Often she would translate the words for me from her school newsletter and the Yiddish newspaper. She even explained the difference between Hebrew and Yiddish. I was impressed and wished I could read Spanish that well.

I could read simple words in Spanish, and often I tried to read the daily Spanish language newspapers. But I missed much of what was written.

Even though we lived in a mixed neighborhood, Jewish families were a minority. There was also a group of four girls who used to make fun of Alberto. They called him the "hallelujah kid" and would refer to Marilyn as "Jew girl." One was also Puerto Rican but claimed her parents had really been born in Spain. She insisted that her fair skin and blond hair were proof enough. The other one had arrived here as a baby from Cuba. The other two were of Irish and German descent and Italian American.

It upset me to hear them calling my friends names; it hurt my feelings. But I said nothing because part of me also wanted to be around them. These girls were popular; they wore the latest clothes and were admired by the other children. I felt important hanging out with them.

As long as I was able to keep my friendship with Alberto and Marilyn separate from my relationship with these other girls, all was fine.

Then one afternoon I was walking with the four girls, and we saw Marilyn returning home from Hebrew school. She waved and started toward me. "There's your friend, the Jew girl," one of them said. I remember wanting to join Marilyn but not daring to go on ahead. I was too afraid of how these girls might judge me.

Marilyn's wide smile faded when she greeted me and saw my reluctance. "What do you want, Jew girl?" they asked. At once Marilyn became perplexed and angered. She told them she was talking to me. But I just stood there mute, not responding and feeling powerless. Somehow I didn't want to be the underdog this time, I didn't want to be the spick. I was willing to let her be the target of those heartless girls, as long as I could be on the winning side.

Marilyn was carrying her Yiddish newspaper and her books. One of them pointed to her paper and made another disparaging remark, and they shoved her books out from under her arm. My heart sank as I watched, yet I still said nothing. Then Marilyn looked directly at me, and I saw the look of sadness and disbelief cross her face. She didn't need words to tell me that I had betrayed her. I already knew what I had just done.

When Marilyn started to pick up her books, one of the girls kicked them out of her reach. As they walked away, I bent down and began to help Marilyn. The other girls called out to me, asking me to join them. I couldn't respond or even look at them. Shame and confusion overwhelmed me. All I could manage was trying to help Marilyn.

"Don't touch my books," Marilyn snapped at me. "I'm proud to be Jewish, so go on with your friends." I tried my best to tell her that they weren't my friends and that these girls meant nothing to me. But she didn't believe me and would not let me help her. The girls continued to shout my name until I waved them off and shook my head.

Then it came, it happened. I heard them yelling to me. "It takes a spick like you to love a Christ killer!" It hurt the most when I understood that the Hispanic girls were also shouting out epithets against me.

I walked alongside Marilyn, who ignored me. No matter how much I pleaded and told her I was sorry and even admitted I was wrong to try to be their friends, Marilyn refused to understand.

Finally I ended up walking home alone and being totally miserable. I felt like a fool when I recalled how I had behaved just to be around those shallow girls. I didn't care how popular they were. I hated them now and wouldn't be their friend even if they begged me. I also knew that all four would probably get on my case. I had to get ready to deal with them and their cruelty. I wasn't afraid of them harming me physically. Growing up with six older brothers and a boy cousin, I had learned how to defend myself. Not too many kids dared to pick a fight with me. It was the power of the girls' popularity and their verbal abuse that frightened me.

The most painful part, though, was losing Marilyn's friendship. Remembering the look on her face made me so remorseful that I couldn't hold back the tears. I learned an important lesson that afternoon, one that would serve me well for the rest of my life.

Marilyn had stood her ground and been proud of who she was. It reminded me of when I was younger and those girls in the all-white neighborhood attacked me. I had not been able to fight back because I was too little and they had all ganged up on me. All I could do was run upstairs, crying for my mother and seeking refuge.

Now that I was older and could have said something, I had remained silent and had not only sold out my good buddy Marilyn, but had also compromised my own values. For what, I asked myself. To be seen with a bunch of superficial fools? If I had been as confident and proud as Marilyn, I would never have wanted any part of those girls in the first place.

I should have spoken up as soon as I heard their verbal abuses toward Alberto and Marilyn. From the beginning I should have made my own position clear. Most importantly, I should have known that those girls could never be my friends. Of course, all of this clarity came after the fact.

I learned a valuable lesson that afternoon, about the value of friendship and self-esteem. I vowed never ever to keep silent again.

Making up with Marilyn was not easy. I tried talking to her several times and walking home with her. Finally, when I decided that I might as well give up, Marilyn broke the ice. She asked me when I was going to the library because she had to find a book there.

I asked why she had changed her mind and was willing to speak to me. Marilyn told me that she had spoken to her parents about the incident. They had told her that since I had admitted the error of my ways, it was now up to her to be generous of spirit and accept my apology.

I thought things would be different and that there would be tension between us. But I guess because we had both survived a breach of trust, things were now clearer than before, and this made for an even better friendship.

Fourteen
....
The Matriarchy Governs

*I*n spite of all of the economic hardship and the responsibility of being a single parent, my mother managed the situation all right. I saw how much she seemed to enjoy her independence.

"It's nice not to have to ask a man for permission," she once told me. I became curious and asked her, permission for what? My mother explained: permission for money, for spending it, to go out with a friend, to buy a piece of furniture—in fact, permission for anything and everything, she told me.

She went on to reveal how much she liked being single in spite of the hardships. She could do as she pleased and make her own independent decisions. My mother was her own boss now and would never remarry, she said, because she preferred it this way.

After sharing with me how much she missed her native island of Puerto Rico, she went on to disclose that she could not go back to live there. The main reason was that she had been able to claim her independence as a woman and as a widow in New York City. In Puerto Rico, this independence would not be hers so easily, especially without financial security.

"Women have a greater chance at personal freedom here," she told me. "A woman can be her own person. No one would judge her in this large city." She didn't have to worry about her reputation if she were seen in the company of a man.

My mother came from a patriarchal culture, where she felt her life would be defined by male dominance and her choices would be limited. Now she was free to go anywhere she pleased without being harassed by accusations and the gossip of her neighborhood. It was an autonomy she valued and did not ever want to relinquish.

Still, my mother longed for the beauty of her island, for the language and enrichment of her people. Like so many of her countryfolk, my mother craved for a plot of earth in the land of her birth, a place where she could grow fresh vegetables and flowers. But there was no money for such a dream. At the same time, my mother acknowledged the prejudice that *we* as Puerto Ricans had to face in New York City. She fully understood that many opportunities were being denied to us simply because of our ethnicity. However, as a woman alone, without economic means, who treasured her personal independence, she felt that New York City was the better alternative.

I observed that she was right, because I had never before seen her as content and as confident. She handled her independence with ease and optimism.

My mother was an accepting and gracious host. Lots of people came by to visit us in our apartment, and they were always greeted with kindness. My friends, my brothers' friends, and an assortment of folks that not everyone would receive into their home were welcomed in ours.

One was a man called America, who was effeminate and homosexual. She warned us not to make fun of him when he wore lipstick and powder, or when he spoke about his late *marido,* husband, who had recently passed away. We were told that America could not help himself, that he was one of God's children and just as valuable as the rest of us. America was always pleasant and often brought me a small present of a sachet, nail polish, or a small bottle of toilet water.

In addition to friends and relatives, we had a neighbor who became our adopted great uncle.

There were only two apartments on a floor, and he occupied the flat right next door to us. Mr. Leon Meyerson lived all alone, having worked most of his life as a salesman of men's clothing in the garment center of Manhattan in order to support his widowed mother and five younger sisters. He often bragged about how he had married each and every sister to a businessman or a professional.

Mr. Meyerson never married. He devoted himself to the care of his mother, who had died just before we moved in. He often lamented how his sisters never came to see him. When they did come, they pleaded over and over with him to move out of the old apartment. They promised to set him up in a better neighborhood, but Mr. Meyerson refused to move. He told them that he was used to Prospect Avenue because he knew the neighborhood and his synagogue was right around the corner.

The first time he came to visit, he brought a paper sack containing a jar of herring in sour cream, an apple, a few grapes, and several slices of pumpernickel bread. He asked if he could put his food in our refrigerator because he had shut off the one in his apartment. He had very little food and saw no need to use unnecessary electricity.

Despite the fact that our small refrigerator could barely hold food for all of our family, my mother would not dream of refusing him. Actually, he only used our refrigerator two or three times. I think this was Mr. Meyerson's way of inviting himself into our home. He walked with a limp, supporting himself against a sturdy wooden cane, and always wore his yarmulke indoors.

It was shortly after his first visit that he became a member of the family. At the beginning, during that first visit, he told my mother that he had become very religious after his retirement and ate only kosher food. My mother replied that her food was very clean and that each Sunday she prepared a specialty called Puerto Rican chicken. She insisted he eat with us. She assured Mr. Meyerson that the chicken was kosher and convinced him by explaining that he was too skinny and needed nourishment. My mom stressed that his own dear departed mother would want us to care for him.

Mr. Meyerson needed very little convincing and soon joined us each and every Sunday for dinner. He'd wear a starched white shirt, a tie, colorful suspenders, and a fancy embroidered velvet yarmulke. What Mr. Meyerson was eating was not chicken. In fact, it was my mother's delicious roast pork and yellow rice with red beans. She warned us that we were not to say a word about the food to Mr. Meyerson, and we knew she meant business.

I can still see Mr. Meyerson, his yarmulke falling to the side of his bald head as he grasped his cane while napping in our old armchair. Or he would be sitting at our kitchen table, content to watch my mother fix him a cup of herbal tea. He enjoyed telling us stories about when he and his family had arrived in this neighborhood forty years earlier. There were horses and buggies then and no elevated trains or traffic, he told us. It was all farm country, and the air was fresh and clean.

Like many old people, he was lonely and alone. His eccentricities, like repeating himself or imagining that we were talking about him, were easily ignored. We were all used to our aunt Maria, and so Mr. Meyerson's peculiarities paled by comparison.

It was humorous when the two of them got together to have a conversation. Aunt Maria barely spoke English, and both she and Mr. Meyerson were hard of hearing and quite stubborn. When one couldn't get a point across, the other became indignant and threatened to leave. My mother was always the peacemaker who turned the situation into an amusing episode.

Now as I recall our relationship with Mr. Meyerson, I suspect that it didn't matter to him about the food he was fed or keeping kosher. The love and sense of family he received from all of us were blessings that transcended religious dogma.

In my second book, *El Bronx Remembered,* a collection of short stories and a novella, one of the stories is based on this childhood experience. It's titled "Mr. Mendelsohn." The story may be fiction, but the feelings and bonding between the old man and the family are all true.

Our friends were always welcomed in my mother's home, and another plate was quickly set at the table. My mother managed to stretch food so that no one ever went away hungry. Despite economic hardship and family squabbles, I had a happy time for those two years prior to my mother's death. There was laughter and hope.

Perhaps because of all the turmoil, death, and separation that we had endured, I so treasured those times of quiet enjoyment that I shared with my mother. I remember that during the afternoons I would set up my drawing equipment by the rear window of her bedroom. She would be sewing or crocheting, and I would be working on my drawings. Sporty would be by my feet, Missmeow would be on the bed, and I could hear my mother's valued birds chirping in harmony.

Occasionally, my mother would inspect my drawings and tell me how wonderful they all were. "You must always do your work," she would say, "and respect the wonderful gift that God has given you."

It was understood that I was going on to college to study art. No matter what we had to do, my mother impressed upon me that I must continue my education. I never doubted for a moment that I would study art. I had my heart set on attending the High School of Music and Art in Manhattan. It was a special school where the students could major in music or in art.

When I inquired at my junior high school, I was informed that I needed a high grade point average to qualify. Some of the kids told me that if a student did exceptionally well at Music and Art, she might receive a scholarship to go on to study art at any number of colleges in the city. As a result, I had been working hard at school to keep up my grades and hard at home doing my artwork.

Memories of those intervals spent drawing by my mother's side in the cradle of peace and harmony are like precious jewels stored in my memory vault. I take out these recollections now and again, and soak up the happiness my mother and I shared just before it all came to an end.

I don't remember exactly when, but I began to notice that my mother was tired a great deal of the time. She looked pale and complained of pains in her abdomen. Illness was no stranger to my mom. Several times when I was growing up, she had taken sick. On at least four occasions she was hospitalized and twice underwent surgery.

This past year she had gone for radium treatments for a malignancy in her uterus. She was worried about her health and told me that she very much wanted to talk to me about that and a number of other things. I remember the day quite well because it was to be the next to the last serious conversation we had before her death. She was sicker than anyone suspected.

That afternoon it was a clear, crisp autumn day and my mother invited me to join her for a cup of hot chocolate. We sat in the kitchen looking out our fire escape window. We saw fenced-in backyards comprised of green patches. The leaves on the trees and bushes were beginning to turn yellow and orange. Above us, white clouds against a pale aqua sky drifted along at a steady pace.

I was thirteen and a half years old and had already gotten my period. Aunt Maria had informed me that I was now a "virgin" and I was to be very, very careful, especially around boys. But my mother had already warned me many times over that I was not to get involved with a boy and become pregnant. She reminded me of Amy, who had long since left my brother Johnny and made a life of her own. She spoke about the many young women who were forced to raise children by themselves. Being a mother and supporting myself and my child would take up my entire life, she warned.

"I had no choice. I was forced to marry at sixteen. But you have a choice." She cautioned that I would lose my freedom and any hope of a future. "Otherwise, say good-bye to high school, college, and your art career!" I respected my mother; she was a strong and intelligent person. Such warnings did not go unheeded.

We sat watching the marshmallows melt into the warm brown liquid, occasionally sipping the sweet chocolate. My mother was a loving person, and when I reached over and hugged her, she returned my affection and told me how much she loved me. She had waited for a daughter for many years, and with each pregnancy she had always wanted a girl. Now she was happy to have such a smart and talented daughter, she said.

Then she told me the bad news, and it almost made my heart stop beating. She had cancer of the uterus. The good news was that she was going to have a hysterectomy, and hopefully this operation would remove the cancer and restore her health.

She made me promise that no matter what happened, I would go on with my plans. "Promise me that you will go on to be an artist someday just like you planned. Be somebody, *mi hijita,* and have a life that will bring you joy and fulfillment. Let that joy come from within you." I promised her. She hugged me so hard and so long that I could not help but feel her desperation.

Fifteen
....
Sadness and Disappointment Go Hand in Hand

*T*he surgeons opened up my mother and never bothered to operate. The cancer had spread throughout her body; there was no point in going on with the hysterectomy. She was sent home, and the prognosis was that she would last from six months to a year.

When my mother went to the hospital, I was distracted and depressed, and my schoolwork suffered as a result. I was in my last year of junior high school. If I wanted to attend the high school of my choice, I would have to work extra hard to pick up my grades.

The doctors told us that we must keep the news of my mother's condition from her. No one was to say a word about the prognosis. I tried not to think about it and hoped and prayed for a miracle. My brother Petie had joined the Navy, and my brother Georgie was not interested in school and wanted permission to join up as well. But my mother was reluctant to let her youngest son leave the nest. Cousin Ralphy was due to be discharged from the Marines in another year.

My brother Johnny had been let out on parole and quickly violated his freedom. Since then we had only seen him a few times, and it was always when he needed help. He had become a drug addict and lived his life as a criminal. Once he had been ill and my mother nursed him back to health. Another time he asked for money, and twice he had needed a place to stay for a few days.

My mother pleaded incessantly with him to stay home and give up his existence of drug use and of violence, but it was all in vain. Johnny cared for nothing, nor for anyone, except his addiction. My mother had a premonition that she would die and wanted desperately to see her firstborn son. Now that she was seriously ill, we attempted to send Johnny the news.

Vincent made arrangements to come back home to live with us. He was working and going to college at night, and this tragic event disrupted his life. It would take some time before his wife, Nancy, could join him. My brother Gilbert came home from the service, and he and his bride also moved in to live with us. Both my sisters-in-law were lovely young women and did all they could to help out. It was wonderful to have my brothers back at home, although we all had to get used to crowded quarters once more.

My mother was too astute and understood that things had gone wrong for her. She confronted her sons and insisted that she had a right to know. It took a couple of months, but as her condition worsened, she demanded a consultation with the doctors and was finally told the truth.

My mother's younger sister Regina had suffered a nervous breakdown. She had two children to care for and was still nervous and fragile. She was not capable of truly helping out. Distant relatives were sympathetic but had families, problems, and concerns of their own.

When my mother was in good health, things at home ran smoothly. But once she became ill, our household was like a ship without its captain, and there was no one to direct our family. My married brothers and their wives had jobs to go to and problems of their own. Our family had changed. Now there were family units within our own group, and there was no one to lead the way. Because life without our mother was unthinkable, no one truly took command.

As time went on, my mother was in terrible pain and her cries often echoed throughout the apartment. Painkillers served only as temporary relief and kept her groggy a good deal of the time.

I was becoming more stressed out with the pressure of trying to keep focused at school. My girlfriends were all sympathetic and tried to cheer me up. I'd visit them after school or we'd go window-shopping. But ultimately I had to face my mother's illness. Sometimes I dreaded coming home, because I knew that my mother would be in horrible pain and there was nothing I could do to help ease her suffering.

Even my drawing and artwork could no longer console my grief. I'd try to put pencil to paper or take out my watercolors, but there was not one creative thought in my mind. Soon I'd abandon any attempt at artwork.

Everyone at home was on edge. My aunt Maria was becoming more and more paranoid. She'd accuse us of stealing money from her purse or of trying to get into her room despite the many locks on her bedroom door, trunks, and suitcases. At times we'd laugh and joke that it would surely take so much time and effort to rob her that the thief would quickly give up. But sometimes we began to lose our patience and screamed at her unnecessarily.

No one stopped to realize how much anxiety, fear, and confusion my mother's illness was causing our aunt.

My mother had short intervals where she seemed to be getting better. During these times she'd limp around and joke that Mr. Meyerson would have to lend her his cane. Mr. Meyerson continued to visit and remained our loyal friend. The poor man had seen his own mother die of cancer and now he too wept because he was losing his best friend.

When my mother was in good spirits, everyone at home became optimistic. I'd begin drawing again, feeling secure and hopeful that perhaps my mom would be cured. She'd even cook our favorite dishes and receive visitors. Unfortunately there was always a relapse, and subsequently her condition would degenerate.

Thanksgiving was a time of sadness at home. My mother was having a rough interval. We all got together to cook the turkey and, with her instructions, tried to make traditional Puerto Rican dishes. She joined us for the meal but soon became uncomfortable and went back to her bed.

Now the Christmas holidays were coming and we were all sad, since this would most likely be our last Christmas with our mother. My mother must have sensed the dismal atmosphere surrounding her, because she called a family meeting. She had braided her rich black hair, put on some makeup, and chosen one of her good dresses.

Gently and with dignity, she told us that this indeed might be our last Christmas together and she wanted it to be a happy one. If we would all help, she would prepare our meal. It wouldn't be a whole pig, but this would certainly be a wonderful meal, she said. She wanted us to invite all of the family and our friends. "Everyone is invited," she declared, "to celebrate with our family."

Both my brother Peter and Cousin Ralphy got permission to come home on special leave. The one sad note was the absence of Johnny. No matter how many messages we sent, he was no where to be found.

It did turn out to be a wonderful Christmas, and in fact, my mother led the trimming of the tree. With our help and the help of some relatives, she supervised the cooking, and a traditional Puerto Rican meal—right down to the dessert—was served.

All night long people came to visit. We had a few musicians who sang special songs for my mom. Friends narrated folk rhymes and folktales; others recited their own poetry. Some of her Pentecostal neighbors came by and led a prayer for her recovery. My mother had lost a substantial amount of weight and appeared frail, yet she also looked radiant. She was happy and responsive and miraculously appeared free of pain.

The next day we all opened our gifts. My mother thanked us for the best Christmas she said she had ever had. New Year's came and went and still there was no word from my brother Johnny. I remember that his absence was a great sadness for my mother.

At school, I struggled to keep up my average and was barely making my necessary grades. I was easily distracted. Even when I was outside and saw a mother and daughter walking together,

I became depressed. I missed my mother's strength, her energy, and her guidance.

It was already the end of January, and I was going to graduate in June. I was still determined to study art and had made several dates to meet with my guidance counselor at school. However, because there often was no one at home to take care of my mom, I would leave school early or sometimes stay home the entire day. Consequently, these appointments had been canceled.

Finally one afternoon in early February I met with Mrs. Farrell to discuss my application to the High School of Music and Art. She greeted me cordially, told me to sit down, and asked me if I had thought carefully and seriously about which high school I wanted to attend. I was surprised by that question, since I had already made it known to her that I expected to apply to Music and Art. Nonetheless, I made my intentions clear and told Mrs. Farrell that my plans were to graduate from the High School of Music and Art and go on to college to get a degree in fine arts.

Mrs. Farrell reminded me that my grades had been slipping during the past year at school. Except for my close friends and homeroom teacher, I rarely spoke about my mother's illness. But now I told the guidance counselor about my mother's illness and explained that this was the reason for my lower grades. Mrs. Farrell told me she was sorry, but she remained skeptical.

I had always had top grades, I reminded her, except for the past year. Besides, I was only a few points down, and I promised to make them up no matter what. Please, I told her, I really want to go to the high school of my choice.

I clearly remember how she lit up a cigarette and marched back and forth, as if she were deep in thought. She was a tall, handsome woman who was always well dressed. Finally, with a benevolent smile, she informed me that what she was going to tell me was strictly for my own good. She assured me that her decision about my future had come after much thought and concern for my well-being.

In her judgment, the High School of Music and Art was no place for a student like me. I was poor, she reminded me, and if my mother did not survive, the chances of my going on to college were even slimmer than before. No, instead she had chosen a school where I could learn a trade. She decided, she said with a great deal of satisfaction, that I should be a seamstress. This was a skill that would always ensure me some work, she said.

Her own personal seamstress was Puerto Rican, a woman who fixed most of her clothes and even made special dresses for her. She pointed out that the attractive suit she was wearing was made by her valued seamstress. It was a great skill that my people had, she informed me, and I might as well take advantage of this talent.

My heart sank to the pit of my stomach. I hated sewing. I had never sewed. In fact, just the year before my mom had sewn almost an entire apron for me, which was my assignment in home economics class.

I recalled those failed attempts by my mom to teach me embroidery and crocheting when I was little. I was in a state of panic at the thought that I might spend my high school years sewing. It was like facing a nightmare.

Mrs. Farrell continued talking and sounded quite pleased with herself. But I hardly heard her words anymore. I know I interrupted her and pleaded that she not send me to a sewing school. "I can't sew," I implored, "and I hate sewing. Please don't send me there. Please . . ."

Suddenly, I forgot all about my determination to get into the high school of my choice and my plans to study art. Now I became so fearful of being punished that my goals were cast aside. I tried to keep my voice steady, but I lost all control and began to cry.

Mrs. Farrell handed me a tissue, saying that there was no need to cry. If I didn't want to go to that school she'd find me another. She suggested a school that would teach me textile design, or perhaps fashion illustration. These skills would allow me to continue with my art career, she reasoned, and when I got out of school I could easily find a job. Meekly, but with some resolve, I brought up Music and Art again. I asked that she please reconsider, because I was determined to go to college and I'd find a way.

But her response was firm. In her analysis, if she allowed me to go there, I would be taking the place of a student who was definite college material. It was not fair of me, she scolded, to deprive another student of that place. No, she asserted, blind ambition was not a wise way for me to proceed.

There have been several times in my life when I felt that the world was crumbling under me and that I was falling into a dark abyss. This was surely one of those times. It never occurred to me to insist upon my rights and demand a school hearing. I was probably the best artist in my school. Everyone was aware of my abilities. My grades had always been in the top ten percent. Yet I had no knowledge that I could take action against this teacher and fight for my rights. As far as I knew, I had no rights.

There was no way I could go home and complain to my brothers. Everyone was busy tending to my mother. The situation at home was tense at best, and most other times it was chaotic. How could I burden them with this? It would be too selfish. Besides, I was sure it was my fault. I had done something to deserve this decision. I had not worked hard enough— or maybe I just wasn't good enough.

I walked home that gray February day, and I remember the cold drizzle numbing my cheeks as I tried not to cry. I felt ashamed of myself, as if I had let my mother down.

No matter how heartbroken I felt, I decided that I would not tell my mother what had happened. In fact, I was not going to mention it to anyone else, either.

Sixteen
....
Graduation and the Final Good-bye

*A*fter my meeting with my guidance counselor, I lost interest in school, and my grades got worse instead of better. I was dropped from the honors class during my final semester because my average went down drastically, as did my attendance.

I think back and realize how my brother Vincent was dealing with his job, night school, and commuting back and forth to Connecticut. Although he had once been my teacher guiding me along the path of knowledge, understandably he had little time for me or my problems now.

I took no interest in the preparations for the graduation ceremony. Usually I would jump at the chance to do artwork for the auditorium, but now I refused to have anything to do with the planning committee. Since no one at home took notice, I stayed away from school as often as I could. I began to sign my own report cards and took care of any school correspondence that was mailed to my home.

My mother was very ill. Her pain was so great that sometimes I couldn't understand how she held on to life. I believe that my mother stayed alive longer than expected because she was determined to see me graduate from junior high school.

Sick as she was, with the help of my aunts she made me a

beautiful white graduation dress with a matching purse and a ribbon headband. My brothers bought me a bouquet of flowers. On graduation day, my mother was too ill to attend the ceremonies. However, arrangements were made and I had my picture taken by a neighborhood photographer. It is one of the few photos of me when I was a girl.

During the ceremony I was secretly relieved that my mother was not in attendance. Not only had I been dropped from the honors class, but I was receiving no prizes, not even a special mention. If my mother had been present, it would have added to my feelings of humiliation and guilt.

When I got home, my aunts, cousins, relatives, and friends were in attendance. They had all been invited for refreshments. Family and friends had gathered to celebrate. People congratulated me and asked about my plans for an art career.

I could see how happy and proud my mother was, and I forgot all about my own personal misery and responded positively. I assured everyone that I was going ahead with my plans. My conviction to succeed impressed my mother favorably, and I in turn delighted in her happiness.

In spite of my disappointments and self doubts, I was happy to have my mom by my side. That meant more to me than anything else in the world. Feeling her joy and her pride toward me, I too felt, deep down in my soul, that I was going to succeed just like she wanted.

During this long ordeal my mother had been hospitalized twice. These separations caused her to become despondent. She did not want to be away from her loved ones. The decision was made that she would spend her last days in her own home.

Just before she lapsed into a deep coma, my mother had a few days of unexpected tranquility. She sat up and let me brush and braid her beautiful long black hair. Friends and relatives remarked how well my mother looked. My family thought that maybe our prayers had been answered and my mother was getting better.

But it was during that time that she announced that she wanted to talk to all of us individually. I remember that she closed the door to her bedroom and spoke privately with each and every one of us, including my sisters-in-law.

This took two days, and I had to wait my turn because I was the last one to visit her. My mother was in good spirits and asked me to come and sit beside her.

At first, we talked about things in general. We joked about Aunt Maria's latest charge of thievery against some unsuspecting guest. My mother asked me about school and I lied, telling her that I was going to a wonderful high school to study art. I even elaborated about how if I worked hard I could easily get a scholarship and go on to art college.

After an awkward moment of silence, my mother told me that she was not going to live to see me achieve my goals. Her sadness, she said, was not as great as her worry. I would be alone, without parents, at the mercy of others. What if I strayed, she asked, what if I didn't finish school, what was to become of her daughter?

I told her that I loved her and that I'd achieve my goals, but she wasn't completely convinced. Her mood changed, and to my surprise she began to cry. Then she told me why I had to succeed.

She was dying, she said, and had never fulfilled her personal dreams. My mother then asked me to imagine a life of success, doing my artwork, and compare that to a life without my art and without my dreams. "Never forget what you want, never," she said.

In fact, how she had felt about life and her aspirations when she was my age were so dim in her memory that she could no longer remember what these goals were. "A woman cannot live only for others, only for her children," she said. "I know." Her whole life had been devoted to her children, she told me, and here she was watching the living go on without her.

My mother grieved that she was dying without ever having known herself. It was an empty feeling, a void deep inside her being. She made me promise and repeat to her that I would achieve my goals, no matter what.

"Please," she implored, "don't die like me. Please don't die like me." Then she took my hands and kissed them and apologized for any hurt she had ever caused me. She told me that she had given me a better life than she had ever experienced. Although, she maintained, this wasn't enough, nor was it what I deserved, it was the best she could do.

We hugged and cried, and there was one brief moment when I was tempted to ask her about Martin and the truth of my birth. But somehow that subject seemed less important compared to the charge my mother had just handed me.

That was the last real conversation we had. The next day my mother lapsed into a coma. She survived in this state for about a week before she took her last breath and died.

She had lived almost a year and a half after her initial prognosis. My mother was forty-nine years old.

Except for my brother Johnny, all her children attended her funeral.

There are two major components that have helped me survive and thrive. The first was my imagination and the powers of my creative inner life. The second was my mother's faith in me and her determination that I succeed.

The creative mind is a powerful instrument, and I believe we are all born with this gift. I am most grateful that in my life I've been able to use this gift to overcome the pressures of society and the tragedies of my personal life. Consequently, I have been able to succeed in my chosen profession and to share the richness of my culture through the expression of my work.

I continue to search and to learn, for if there is one thing that I have grasped, it is that one is never too old or too young to explore the wonders of one's own imagination.

Epilogue

Åfter my mother's death, I returned to my artwork and found great solace in my drawings and watercolors. I periodically remembered her words and tried to imagine an existence in which I could not use my creative abilities. The thoughts were grim. By contrast, when I imagined my life as an artist I just knew that I would have to pursue my goals.

Upon graduation from junior high school I applied for working papers and got a job as a page girl in the New York Public Library, my favorite home away from home.

In high school I was assigned to study fashion illustration. I concentrated more on watercolor technique and drawing than I did on subject matter. Upon graduation, I enrolled in the Art Students League and began studying art in earnest and under the right circumstances. In time, I saved enough money and went on to study in Mexico City, at the *Taller de Graficos,* for a semester. I returned home and continued my studies at the New School for Social Research, the Brooklyn Museum Art School, and Pratt Graphics Center.

During that time I met my husband, Irwin, who was a doctoral student in clinical psychology. We fell in love, married, and had two sons, David and Jason.

I became a painter and printmaker and achieved a moderate amount of success. My work was included in many exhibits, both nationally and internationally. I was affiliated with galleries in several large cities throughout the United States, including my native city of New York, where I was also being represented by an art agent.

My work contained a lot of graffiti and words. "Your artwork has so many words," my agent told me, "I think you're also a writer." Indeed, some time later, my agent informed me that a collector who was also a publisher had requested that I write about my life experiences growing up.

I was reluctant at first, but my agent became insistent, reminding me that there were no books representing my culture and that I would be filling a void. He was right. At that time, in 1972, there were virtually no books written about or by Puerto Ricans and other Latinos, concerning their lives and experiences. I knew this all too well because I was raising two young sons and could not offer them any books depicting my community in New York City.

With some trepidation, I agreed and wrote fifty pages of vignettes based on my young life. Surprisingly, my agent returned my work, saying that he and the publisher were both dissatisfied and urged me to try again.

But their reasons were offensive to me. They expected me to write about gang wars, sex, violence, and all the negative stereotypes imaginable. Apparently I could not give them what they wanted. My life had been one of study and hard work. I had never been in trouble or confronted society with violence and disorder.

It was shocking that in spite of my talents and education they viewed me as an outsider living apart from the greater society at large. In their view, I was a Puerto Rican woman who could reveal a world of nefarious exploits. I decided never to write another word for them, and I put my vignettes away. Artwork was all they would get from me. In fact, I planned to sever my association with my agent.

A week later, however, Harper & Row called me to ask if I was interested in designing a book jacket for them. I normally worked in the field of fine arts and had little interest in commercial work, but I agreed to show them my portfolio. I didn't do the jacket. Instead, I asked if they would read my vignettes, and they agreed. But they also made it clear that they were in no way committing themselves.

Based on my vignettes, Ellen Rudin, who was then editor in chief at Harper & Row, commissioned me to write a novel. I was not restricted to writing it for any particular age group, but I told the story through the eyes of a young girl between ten and fourteen. Having the creative skills with which to proceed with other artistic endeavors, I took the techniques I knew and transferred them onto the craft of writing. Furthermore, I have always had a natural ability to write.

I also created the book jacket and eight illustrations for the publication of my first book, *Nilda*. In 1973, *Nilda* was published as a young adult book and received much critical acclaim. This book contains a lot of autobiographical material although it is, in fact, fiction.

My second book, *El Bronx Remembered,* a collection of stories and a novella, was published by Harper & Row in 1975. I continued in the two fields of fine arts and writing until 1976, when I dismantled my studio and devoted myself entirely to writing.

My major work continues to be writing. I write for children, young adults, and adults. Although I love writing books, I've also written screenplays, plays, and scripts for television. However, my favorite kind of writing is narrative fiction, and my favorite written art form is the short story.

Now and then, I do artwork using oil crayons, pen and ink, and gouache. But these artworks are not done for professional reasons; they are simply for my own gratification.

Irwin died in 1978 and my sons are now grown.

When my mother died, she left me no material goods or riches. However, her honesty, as expressed in her final words, linger on as beacons directing me to honor my goals and to respect my culture.

I feel fortunate to do work that is fun and creative and that serves as a conduit of communication enabling me to share with others the celebration of our imagination and the creative spirit.

Published Works

·······················

BOOKS, STORIES, AND CHAPTER BOOKS

All for the Better: A Story of El Barrio (Working Together series). Austin, TX: Steck-Vaughn, 1993.

An Awakening . . . Summer 1956 (Woman of Her Word). Houston, TX: Arte Público Press, 1983.

El Bronx Remembered. New York: HarperCollins (hardcover), 1975. Reprint. New York: Bantam (paperback), 1976. Reprint. Houston, TX: Arte Público Press (paperback), 1986. Reprint. New York: HarperTrophy (paperback), 1993.

Felita. New York: Dial Press (hardcover), 1979. Reprint. New York: Bantam Skylark (paperback), 1990. Reprint. New York: Dell Yearling (paperback), 1981.

Going Home. New York: Dial Books for Young Readers (hardcover), 1986. Reprint. New York: Bantam Skylark (paperback), 1989.

Isabel's New Mom (Reading–Theme books). New York: Macmillan, 1994.

Jaime and the Conch Shell (bilingual publication *Tun-Ta-Ca-Tun*). Houston: TX: Arte Público Press, 1986.

Nilda. New York: HarperCollins (hardcover), 1973. Reprint. New York: Bantam (paperback), 1974. Reprint. Houston, TX: Arte Público Press (paperback), 1986.

In Nueva York. New York: Dial Press (hardcover), 1977. Reprint. New York: Dell Publishing (paperback), 1979. Reprint. Houston, TX: Arte Público Press (paperback), 1988.

Rituals of Survival: A Woman's Portfolio. Houston, TX: Arte Público Press, 1985.

A Special Gift (KIKIRIKI). Houston, TX: Arte Público Press, 1981.

Uncle Nick's Gift (Passages). New York: Holt, Rinehart & Winston Inc., 1988.

JOURNAL ARTICLES, PAPERS, AND MAGAZINE ARTICLES

"The Journey Toward a Common Ground: Hispanics in the U.S.A." *Americas Review* (1990).

"Puerto Rican Writers in the United States, Puerto Rican Writers in Puerto Rico: A Separation Beyond Language." *Americas Review* (1992).

"A Personal Odyssey into Fiction." *Writers Speak: America and the Ethnic Experience* (Institute for Advanced Study in the

Humanities at the University of Massachusetts at Amherst, 1984).

"Puerto Ricans in New York: Cultural Evolution and Identity." *Imagenes e Identidades: El Puertorriqueno en la Literatura,* Ediciones Huracan, Puerto Rico (1985).

"Puerto Ricans in the U.S.: The Adopted Citizen." *Ethnic Lifestyles and Mental Health* (Oklahoma State University Psychology Department, Stillwater, Oklahoma, 1978).

ANTHOLOGIES

Nicholasa Mohr's work appears in many anthologies, including the following:

Breaking the Boundaries. University of Massachusetts at Amherst, 1989.

To Break the Silence. Dell Publishing, 1986; MCP Literature Program, 1987.

The Ethnic American Woman: Problems, Protest, Lifestyles. Kendall/Hunt, 1984.

Imagining America. Persea Books, 1991.

Passages. Holt, Rinehart, Winston, Inc., 1989.

Women on War. Touchstone Books, 1988.

Aguas Tranquillas. Economy Spanish Reading Series, The Economy Co., 1987.

Women of the Century. St. Martin's Press, 1993.